S0-ADS-653

Fame or Fortune

Fame or Fortune

✦

Giants of the housing industry revealed

Ned Eichler

iUniverse, Inc.
New York Lincoln Shanghai

Fame or Fortune
Giants of the housing industry revealed

Copyright © 2005 by Ned Eichler

All rights reserved. No part of this book may be used or reproduced by any means, graphic, electronic, or mechanical, including photocopying, recording, taping or by any information storage retrieval system without the written permission of the publisher except in the case of brief quotations embodied in critical articles and reviews.

iUniverse books may be ordered through booksellers or by contacting:

iUniverse
2021 Pine Lake Road, Suite 100
Lincoln, NE 68512
www.iuniverse.com
1-800-Authors (1-800-288-4677)

ISBN-13: 978-0-595-36734-4 (pbk)
ISBN-13: 978-0-595-81155-7 (ebk)
ISBN-10: 0-595-36734-8 (pbk)
ISBN-10: 0-595-81155-8 (ebk)

Printed in the United States of America

Contents

Introduction

In 1948, I was eighteen years old and a sophomore at Dartmouth College. I began working for my father during summer vacations. Like a great many other Americans at the time, he had entered a business that was foreign to them and to him. He was building houses for sale in a tract of fifty lots in Sunnyvale, California. During that and two successive summers, I performed the tasks of an unskilled laborer—planting lawns, driving a truck, and carrying lumber for a framing crew. By the time I graduated in 1951, my father had switched the style of the houses he was building from conventional to modern construction and had achieved local and even national fame for doing so. I had learned enough about the special materials required for these new designs to take on the job of purchasing them.

For the next twelve years, I remained ambivalent about engaging in the process. My father and the many others like him who became what I later called "merchant builders" were fully committed to business as an occupation. I was not. I was, in part, an intellectual, one who is committed to ideas, to a life of the mind. Nevertheless, for several reasons, I undertook the task. First, it was almost certain that soon I would be drafted into the Army. Second, I had ideas about how to improve the nature of the materials that were endemic to an Eichler home and the method of delivering them. Third, like my father and other merchant builders, I was attracted to a key aspect of the activity: it was not technical or artificial. Fourth, as I shall show in greater detail, my father's determination to build inexpensive, architect-designed, modern houses was infectious. We were involved in the business not to just make money, although that was a necessary objective, but to pursue a larger cause.

A year later, in June 1952, I was drafted into the Army. Fortunately, after an abbreviated basic training, followed by some special instruction in cryptography, I was sent to Germany for a few months and then to the center of Paris for another year. During those two years in the Army, I became increasingly conflicted about whether or not I should return to the business. I seriously considered being discharged in Paris and traveling around Europe as a freelance journalist and perhaps a writer of fiction like that of Somerset Maugham and

Graham Greene, but then and long after, I remained torn between going my own way or rejoining my father. Part of the attraction to do the latter was negative, a desperate desire to gain what I never had and never would get—my father's concern for me as a person.. But I was seduced by my love and respect for him and for what he was trying to do. He often quoted adages from Shakespeare. My dilemma fit one of those, "The wish is father to the thought."

So I went back to work at Eichler Homes and stayed there for the next ten years, during which I did some very constructive work, some of which I subsequently applied to a business of my own. I also met many other merchant builders, most of whom I respected and some of whom I found fascinating as characters. Later, I wrote a book about the process. In 1964, I was so disillusioned with the course my father had chartered for his company that I left to run a Ford Foundation—financed study of new towns at the University of California at Berkeley and to teach there as well. As I shall describe in a subsequent chapter, this led to writing my first book. After the company went bankrupt in 1967, I had no money, was getting a divorce, and had to make a living. I tried three short jobs, and in 1973 I joined Victor Palmieri Company (VPCO) to manage the disposition of the real estate of the bankrupt Pennsylvania Railroad. It was in this capacity that I met and spent as much as half my time for a year negotiating with Donald Trump. In 1975, VPCO was appointed by a federal court to restructure what had been the largest merchant building firm in the country, Levitt and Sons. As the only partner at VPCO who had home-building experience, I became Levitt's acting president. I soon realized that by my temperament and experience, I was well-suited to dealing with the problems that arose from others' gross mismanagement.

I had moved to New York to work for VPCO, but when it was over in 1980, I returned to the Bay Area, taught again at UC–Berkeley, and wrote *The Merchant Builders*, which was published by MIT Press. After two years of exploring alternatives and again needing to make some money, by an accident I engaged in what was for me a new activity—originating and servicing loans on existing rental projects, the only business I ever founded. As I shall explain later, the combination of being an outsider and an intellectual and my experiences at Eichler Homes helped me to structure and manage this business. Concurrently, I returned to a long held and unsatisfied interest, the study of history. From 1984 to 1988, I took all of the courses required in the PhD program at the history department at UC–Berkeley. I preferred simply to pick and choose courses, but the department chairman insisted that I choose a specific area and time period.

Reluctantly, I selected modern (1789–present) Europe and then shifted to the United States.

I had taught previously in business schools. I expected that students and teachers of history would be far more interested in general ideas than their counterparts studying business. With one or two exceptions, this turned out to be an unrealistic assumption. The students were obsessed with carving out a narrow career niche, and the interests of most professors were equally myopic. As I was completing the course work, I decided to write a book about what was then a very hot topic: the plight of savings and loans and savings banks, or what were called thrifts. In the early 1980s, they had been deregulated in most respects with one crucial exception: federal insurance for deposits remained. The excessive risks they had taken led to massive losses, which had to be borne by the government. It was, as a former regulator said, the worst financial disaster in American history. In my book, *The Thrift Debacle*, I traced the path of these institutions since they were founded in the United States in 1816 and stated why they had gone so wrong.

I continued to run my mortgage banking operation in a slightly different form until 1996, at which time I retired not only from it but also from business, writing, and teaching. A small incident earlier in 2005 caused me to consider writing one more book, to which I have given the title *Fame or Fortune*. A friend called me one night and asked, "Did you know you are in a movie called *Trump Unauthorized*?" I replied that I had no idea what she was talking about. I soon learned that ABC had run such a movie and that an actor played me in a short early scene.

As I mentioned before, I had had extensive dealings with Trump in 1973 and 1974, and I had briefly met with him many years later. With much difficulty, I obtained a DVD of the movie and watched it. The movie demonstrated what I had already believed is the underlying meaning of Trump's career: seeking fame for its own sake. Then I wondered how this compared with many other men I had known, whose business was building housing for sale or rent. My father and Bill Levitt, for example, became the only two home builders in the 1950s to gain national fame for their respective achievements. Others had sought publicity about themselves to market their product or sell their companies. Still others were determined to retain their privacy. My choice of the word *fortune* is intentional, but I use it to mean more than making money. For me, it includes additional aspects, such as family, travel, and recreation. In other words, it entails a balanced life. I knew that, in those terms, the lives of Trump, my father, and Bill Levitt had been failures. I did not know how close to success other men whom I knew had gotten. I decided to find the answer to that question and to present the stories of both the successes and the failures of a set of fascinating men with whom I have worked or have known. This book, therefore, is about them and about me.

1

The Setting: Merchant Building

Bill Levitt and Joe Eichler were members of a large group of businessmen who capitalized on a special set of conditions that were in place after World War II. I call the activity in which they engaged "merchant building." It entails buying a large parcel of land, preparing a plan to subdivide it into residential lots, designing the roads and utilities, gaining approval from local governmental authorities for these plans, installing the roads and utilities, building houses on the lots, and selling them for occupancy. There was nothing new about these steps. Each of them had been taken in the United States and elsewhere for centuries. Many of the Founding Fathers, including George Washington, bought large chunks of land for future sale. What was new were scale, comprehensiveness, and the circumstances that made them possible.

The number of housing units built in America before 1946 peaked in 1925 at nine hundred and twenty-five thousand. From then it declined steadily until 1930, when it sank below one hundred thousand. There was a modest increase for the next eleven years until the country entered World War II, during which private home construction all but stopped. When the war ended, therefore, there was tremendous pent-up demand for housing, but that demand was made effective only by the existence of four other favorable conditions. First, the general economy was strong; second, there was readily available, low-cost, high loan-to-value financing for home construction and purchasing; third, there was a major federal effort to construct a network of roads and highways that would make increased amounts of land available for settlement and facilitate commuting; and fourth, there was a general climate of support for the rapid expansion of metropolitan areas, not just by prospective home owners and retail providers but also by state and local governmental authorities. In 1946, all these conditions were in place for the first time anywhere in the world.

There had previously been a few isolated efforts at tract home building, and there had been those who specialized in one function—for example, land subdividers, house builders, mortgage companies, and real estate brokers—but there had never been companies that could fully capitalize on this situation. Because American society had always been favorable to business, expansion, physical and social mobility, and risk taking, it was inevitable that entrepreneurs would emerge to seize the opportunity. I call those opportunists merchant builders. There had been many other historical examples of men founding businesses to take advantage of some new circumstance—for example, using steam to power ships, railroad trains, and looms, building cars powered by combustion engines, or making household appliances powered by electricity. But all these activities and many others depended on advances in technology. Merchant builders rarely possessed any technical knowledge or aptitude, nor had most them had experience with any of the functions involved.

The men who undertook this activity did not, as I do, conceptualize their approach. Had they been prone to do so, they might have said that they asked three questions about the traditional process of getting a parcel of raw land, say 100 acres, developed to the point that there were occupied houses on it. First, what are the steps and how many are there? Second, how many of these steps are unnecessary? And third, how many could be taken concurrently rather than consecutively? The conclusions they reached convinced them that they could greatly improve the process in both direct cost and in time elapsed. The latter was of special importance to men with limited capital, which was the case with most merchant builders at the time.

Even if half the traditional steps were theoretically unnecessary, not all of them could be eliminated. Arbitrary rules of lenders and/or government authorities and ingrained habits of subcontractors and material suppliers could not always be overcome. But most merchant builders who succeeded were relentless in trying to streamline their operations to reduce direct costs, spread overhead, and conserve capital. One of their major aims was to reduce or eliminate their dependence on expensive equity investment by a combination of accumulating earnings and accelerating the entire process. Furthermore, the more volume they achieved, the better chance they had to convince owners to finance land sales.

By 1950, merchant builders were operating in all major metropolitan areas, but there were wide variations in what price range each chose and in annual unit production. All things being equal, the higher the price the lower the volume, but there were other variables such as the size of the market area, climate, and the drive and skill of the operator. Even in the same market and same price range, some builders had more ambition and a wider span of personal control than others. With rare exceptions, especially in the earlier years, builders were far less concerned with fancy architecture than with getting designs that eliminated every possible impediment to reducing direct costs and time required for construction. Most of them subcontracted all the construction operations except carpentry, but with the carpentry and even the subs they constantly worked to break the process down into smaller segments so that workers could specialize. The site was their factory where they organized an assembly line. Similarly, over time many merchant builders brought sales, loan processing, and marketing in-house. The best part of the country in which to gain volume was the West, especially California, where the climate was temperate and the demand from people migrating was the greatest. But there was another variable: competition. A talented and driven merchant builder might do better in the suburbs of Chicago or New York or even Cleveland than in California because there were fewer competitors and they were inferior in ability and in motivation. One of the greatest myths about merchant building in the first two decades after World War II is that it was easy to sell houses and make money. There was a substantial increase in overall volume. By 1950, the annual national rate of housing starts was over two million, about half of which was single family housing. Furthermore, down payments on VA, FHA, and conventional bank loans were reduced and the term was extended. But builders constantly faced two problems. First, there were recurrent cycles of economic activity and of interest rates. Second, there was very easy entry into the business. In other words, merchant building was both highly competitive and inherently cyclical. To make matters worse, when a builder was selling his houses well, it might rain or snow. Unfortunately his factory was in the open, at least until he could get utilities, roads, roofs, and outside walls installed. Ike Jacobs, a colorful and successful Dallas merchant builder, once described the situation as follows: "Every morning the suppliers, the subcontractors, the bank and city inspectors, and the workers have a meeting to figure out how to stop me from getting my houses built. When they can't do that, the prospects decide not to buy. And if none of those efforts succeed, God makes it rain."

Jews represented less than 5 percent of the American population, but although they did not dominate the field as much as they did movies, radio, and television, investment banking, or department stores, a disproportionate percentage of merchant builders were Jewish. Although it was by its nature a private, local activity, by the late 1950s it took on a certain glamour, and some observers wondered if there would be a national home-building company, a "General Motors" of housing. Despite the many limitations, the most obvious of which were that the prod-

uct was attached to a site and climate and tastes varied by region, the fad persisted
and captured the imagination, not only of the general public but also of investment bankers and managers of large industrial corporations. They thought it was
time for this scattered industry to be rationalized. Some merchant builders themselves caught the bug and took their companies public; that is, offered stock for
sale, while others decided the better route was selling to established national
firms, most of them in unrelated activities.

The first two public offerings by merchant builders, Eichler Homes and Levitt
and Sons, were small and had less to do with cashing out than with ego and
opportunity. The founders, Joseph Eichler and William Levitt, were already
famous, one for building houses of modern design in the San Francisco Bay Area
and the other for building complete communities in New York and New Jersey.
They were followed by a few dozen merchant builders, who were seeking access
to cheaper capital but preferred to retain control. Others, more interested in taking advantage of what a few cynics (some would substitute realists) called "suck-
ers," saw a chance to sell their companies to an insurance company, a wood
products manufacturer, a paper products maker, an avowed conglomerate, or
some other large company whose managers were certain they could use their
stock, which was selling at very high multiples of earnings, to acquire these
archaic, local operations and apply their financial resources and managerial expertise to take them national. The head of a Los Angeles–based accounting firm that
specialized in real estate operations, Kenneth Leventhal, once told a client who
was uncertain whether he would accept a multimillion-dollar offer from W.R.
Grace, "I wouldn't give you a quarter for your company. Now let's just get on a
plane, go to New York, and take that money from Grace before they change their
minds."

Knowing that prospective buyers wanted them to expand geographically,
between 1968 and 1973 fourteen merchant builders who decided to sell or go
public added from two to twelve metropolitan areas to their operations. By doing
so, they increased annual unit production dramatically, by 75 to 400 percent.
Several of them also diversified by building commercial and rental projects, the
latter often utilizing newly enacted federal rent subsidies. With two glaring exceptions, Levitt and Eichler Homes, in the same five years they increased stated earnings by even greater percentages. They contended that it had only been the lack
of access to patient capital, not difficulties with span of control that prevented
them from taking these steps. It is impossible now to determine the degree to
which they believed this contention.

Certainly neither the merchant builders nor the buyers of their companies or of their stock took fully into account three factors that would soon make it harder to make a profit. The first was cyclicality. In 1973, the United States economy entered its worst recession since the 1930s. The second was the overbuilding that occurred in late 1960s and early 1970s. The third was the emergence of the environmental movement. Two of them had a negative effect on sales and rental volume and on prices and rents; the other raised land and construction costs. As a result, there was dive in stock prices—from June 1971 to November 1974, for ten companies they fell on average by over 60 percent—and there were several divorces, in which mergers were unwound by the sellers buying back their companies at a fraction of what they had been paid, and, as cited above, bankruptcies. The one exception to this pattern was Larwin, a southern California merchant builder founded in 1946 by Larry Weinberg and sold in an exchange of stock to CNA in 1969 for an initial price of $100 million and an earnout (bonus) of another $100 million based on profits over the next five years. In 1974, Larwin met the earnings target and Weinberg got his second payment.

Weinberg grew up in New Jersey and was injured fighting in World War II. Wanting to complete college, unwilling to enter his father's clothing business, and still needing medical treatment, he went to UCLA. Soon thereafter, he began looking for a business in which he could invest the $10,000 stake he had and settled on merchant building. He began operating in the San Fernando Valley. By 1950, Larwin (the name he selected for his company) was building about 500 houses per year northwest of Los Angeles and turning an excellent profit, but he was worried. During World War II, the government had shut down all private home building. He was certain that with the onset of the Korean War, this would happen again. To make sure he would have a business to own and operate, he purchased out of bankruptcy a small company that made airplane wings. When home building was not banned, he ran both companies for a while and both did well, but he decided to sell the aircraft company. Asked why he made that choice, he said, "Making wings required adherence to design criteria which I did not and could not fully understand and therefore could not question. This is not true with home building. Very little is so technical that I don't feel comfortable challenging an engineer, an architect, a subcontractor, or an inspector about it. Furthermore, there is a lot more to it than just construction, like buying land, getting houses designed, securing zoning, pricing, marketing, selling, arranging financing for myself and for the customers, and processing and closing their loans. I do all that myself or through people I hire and supervise. It is all just common sense and trial and error." By 1969, Larwin was profitably building about three thousand houses per year in and around Los Angeles, San Diego, and the San Francisco Bay Area. I shall devote an entire chapter to Weinberg later.

Some merchant builders like Don Bren and Bill Lyon sold out for a lot of money, bought the business back at a deep discount, and continued running it. Many of them remained private, succeeded, and, in some cases, brought children into the business to ensure its longevity. Others took their companies public, went through bad times for several years, and then gradually began another ascent. In the last fifteen years, a number of regional merchant builders went public and prospered. For the first time in history in 2001, home building did not lead the economy into a recession. In fact, it kept the recession from being more than a blip and boomed thereafter. In the concluding chapter I shall speculate on whether this represents a permanent change and, if it does, what the consequences might be. In any event, this treatise is not mainly about merchant building's role in the overall economy or about its future, but about the character of some of the men who have engaged in it, of builders and owners of rental projects, of Victor Palmieri who prospered by working out major problems, and of Donald Trump.

2

Zealot for Modernity: Joseph Eichler

I knew all the men depicted here but certainly not as well as I knew my father, Joseph Eichler. In fact, I came to understand his complex character better than anyone else, even his wife of fifty years, Lillian, and his eldest son and my brother, Richard. He was born in Manhattan in 1900, the first of three children of Jewish parents who had recently emigrated, the mother from Germany and the father from Austria. They had started a small toy store on 57th Street. His mother, whom he respected and adored, ran the store until she died when he was sixteen. He went to public schools and then to NYU, where he joined a fraternity, had friends with whom he kept some relationship throughout his life, and greatly enjoyed many of his classes. In the first four years after graduating, he held a series of apparently unsatisfying jobs with small investment counselors. In 1925, he married and soon thereafter moved with his new wife to San Francisco to work for her family's wholesale butter and egg business, a job in which he remained for the next twenty years. This brief history demonstrates that my father's life was quite different from that of Donald Trump, Bill Levitt, Larry Weinberg, or most merchant builders.

For reasons I have never been able to fathom, my maternal grandfather, whom my father always referred to as the "Old Man," prospered very quickly. He and a partner founded a business brokering butter and eggs at which they grew quite rich. After only a few years the family bought a house in a Bronx neighborhood, where most of the residents were Irish, and soon after that bought a car. None of the children who survived, except the youngest, George, who became a lawyer, went to college. The eldest, Abe, took over the business when his father died. When a wholesale client in San Francisco went broke and could not pay them, the Old Man and his partner assumed ownership of their business, Nye and Nissen, and soon turned it around. In 1925, he, his partner, and the Moncharsch family, except one daughter who had married, moved to San Francisco. As is not uncommon, an unplanned occurrence had changed the course not only of a business but also of the members of the family who owned it, as well as a new addition to that family, Joseph Eichler, who had recently married Lillian. In 1928 and 1930, respectively, the Eichlers' two sons, Richard and I, were born.

Until 1936, we lived in a rented flat in San Francisco and then moved to a small, Spanish-style home in San Mateo, twenty miles south of the "city." My father later told me that he had bought the home for $10,000 with the aid of two mortgages, which from the outset he yearned to be able to repay. Six years later, after Americans had entered World War II, he came home and announced that we were moving to a home in an upscale adjacent town, Hillsborough. He had rented it from an Air Force pilot, who was away fighting in the war. When I first saw it, I was stunned. It was even smaller than the house in which we had been living, and except for the concrete floors, it was built entirely of wood. This included folding wood shutters in the sleeping alcoves and many built-ins. All of those and all the rooms were shaped octagonally. I later learned that its architect was Frank Lloyd Wright.

Ever since then I have tried to figure out where my father got his interest in modern architecture, of which this house was the first manifestation. The furnishings of our previous home were entirely traditional. There were not even any books on the subject present. I can only suggest five characteristics of his that might be clues. First, he was addicted to whatever was new, such as having a car with an airflow engine or a machine that was supposed to restore hair (he became almost bald early). Second, he liked to read the fiction of contemporary authors like O'Hara, Marquand, Steinbeck, and Cheever. Third, he had no interest in his family's European origins, although he often told me stories about his childhood in New York. Fourth, he was contemptuous of traditions of any kind, including Christmas or Jewish holidays. We never went to temple, and I was barely conscious of being a Jew. Fifth, he was very meticulous about his attire. He had his suits, slacks, sport coats, and overcoats made to order at Brooks Brothers and composed ensembles of them with neckties, hats, socks, and a hat. He admired athletes like Bobby Jones and Joe DiMaggio for their physical grace, which he did not have, but his real hero, both for his dancing and the way he dressed, was Fred Astaire.

But these qualities cannot by themselves account for his passion for modern architecture. I think the answer lies in an inchoate yearning to find some activity in which he could be the dominant actor and through which he could express his nature. He was quite literate and often quoted Shakespeare to make a point—"The wish is father to the thought" or "Sufficient to the day is the evil thereof"—but I never saw him read his plays or sonnets. He was not an intellectual and never tried to write prose or poetry. He had no interest in classical music but sang verses of Gilbert and Sullivan. He must have been bitter about the time he had wasted in the prosaic activities of a business he neither owned nor ran. When the family business was sold in 1945, it left him with only a modest amount of money, no job or even the prospect of one, and no clear idea of what he would do. Then the Air Force officer came home from the war and wanted to reoccupy the Wright house. Now he did not even know where the family would live. He must have been apprehensive, but he may also have felt liberated.

He bought a six-unit building in San Francisco, and we moved into one of the apartments. Then he began to search for a business in which to invest. Soon he was approached by two young engineers who were building components to be assembled into a house on the buyer's lot. Their plant was in Sunnyvale, forty miles south of San Francisco. They needed a few thousand dollars and offered him a partnership if he would provide the funds. He agreed and began driving to their plant two or three days a week to see how things were going. My father soon decided that his partners were incompetent and bought them out. Within a few months, a real estate broker said to him, "Joe, you shouldn't be fooling around with building one house at a time on someone else's lot. You should buy some land, develop it, and build houses on it for sale."

"Where the hell would I get the land, and who would lend me the money for all this?" my father caustically asked. Of course, the broker just happened to have a parcel for sale and a bank to recommend. Soon thereafter, Joe Eichler became a merchant builder.

His first tract consisted of fifty lots in Sunnyvale, where he built houses and sold them for under $10,000. On one of the lots he built a slightly larger home for us. He made only a few minor deviations from the standard, conventional houses of the time. Before all this happened, he had bought a lot in Hillsborough and hired a young architect, Robert Anshen, a disciple of Frank Lloyd Wright, to design a house for it. Anshen's plan was always too expensive, but he and my father continued meeting to try to shave the costs. One of those meetings was held in a tract house that my father had converted into a temporary office. After yet another unsuccessful meeting, my father walked with Anshen to his car, and the architect said, "Goddamn it, Joe, how can someone with your taste build this crap?"

Far from cowed, my father replied, "Jesus, Bob, I sell these houses for under $10,000 and you can't design a house for me that I can build for less than $100,000."

Anshen snapped back, "What the hell has that got to do with it? The closets for your wife's clothes take up more space than one of these houses. Pay me $2,500 to design three models for you that are as big and have the same features as this stuff you're building now and that you can sell for the same price."

My father glared at him for a few moments, turned to walk back to his office, and, without removing from his mouth the ever-present cigar, growled, "Do it." That was the birth of the more than ten thousand "Eichlers" that my father built over the next twenty years.

The houses Anshen designed were 1,000 square feet with three bedrooms and one bath, and they sold for $9,900 in a forty-nine-unit tract in Sunnyvale. The living room and master bedroom had floor-to-ceiling glass walls with sliding glass doors facing the rear of the 6,000-square-foot lot. The exterior and interior walls were covered in redwood, siding for the former and plywood sheets for the latter. The roof frames were constructed by placing ten-inch to fourteen-inch beams six or more feet apart over posts. These were overlaid with tongue-and-groove, two-inch-thick and eight-inch-wide decking, also redwood. The decking was overlaid with insulation and tar and gravel. The floors were four-inch concrete slabs covered by vinyl tile. Radiant heat pipes were embedded in the concrete. Unlike Levitt's radiant heat system, which carried electrically heated tubing, these pipes circulated water that was heated by a gas furnace. The reason for this substitution was the difference between the relative costs of electricity and natural gas in the respective locations. Not only did the houses sell well, but many of the buyers came from Palo Alto and Menlo Park, which were ten miles north, and were overqualified financially. Levitt was selling houses to working-class and lower-middle-class families in Long Island for prices two to three thousand dollars less than this. Most of my father's buyers were middle-class. I later described purchasers of Eichler Homes as having upper-middle-class tastes but lower-middle-class incomes.

Streamlining Construction

The profit margins on these initial Eichler homes were minimal, but my father was determined not only to make a decent profit on his houses but also to be able to build them so efficiently that in features and square footage they could be priced equally with conventional competition, all at a respectable profit. In other words, he would not ask a prospect for an Eichler home to pay a premium for their superior design. He did, however, decide to shift his targeted location north to Palo Alto, where lot costs were slightly higher than in Sunnyvale. For the next six years it was his principal place of operations and soon the location of his office, but he always stuck to his goal of keeping his prices equal in all respects to those of his local competitors.

There was little, if any difference between the cost of materials of a house with a wood subfloor, stucco siding, sheetrock interior walls and ceilings, shingle roof covering, forced-air heating, and smaller glass areas and those in an Eichler home. The main factor causing a modern house to cost more than a conventional one was labor. It required not only more work by carpenters but also more skill. This was the inherent obstacle he had to overcome. His approach was simple. He subdivided carpentry into a series of operations, each to be performed by the same workmen from house to house. What had to be determined was the size of the crew for each operation that would be needed to perform its assigned task in one day or a half a day. This would allow him to drive around any job at the end of the day and tell if everything was working right. The number of workers depended on the complexity of the tasks such as layout, framing, beam installation, roof decking, fascia, siding, exterior trim, door hanging, paneling, or interior trim and hardware. Each crew, even if, as in the case of fascia or layout, it had only two men, had a foreman, who was paid more than union scale. As much as possible, not only did workmen have to perform the same task every day, but there had to be enough volume to keep them busy for at least nine months per year, the dry period in the Bay Area.

This system was largely in place by 1951, when I graduated from college. During summer vacations I had worked at a variety of tasks, from installing lawns to driving a truck and being a laborer for frame and roof crews. Now my father asked me to try to solve a major problem. Our method for procuring materials was far less efficient than it was for performing the carpentry work. Furthermore, there were some functional problems with some of the materials we were using, especially redwood. For interior paneling it was too dark and too soft. So we switched to Philippine mahogany but had logs shipped to Japan for milling because the workmanship was better there. We substituted fir for siding and beams because it was less expensive and lighter. We kept using redwood for roof decking but got mills to alter the standard "construction heart" grade to eliminate the normal 15 percent allowance for short boards and loose knots. This resulted in an "Eichler" grade, which had all tight knots and no short lengths. For the beams, we gave a specific takeoff for each house plan and had a San Francisco lumber company cut them to size and ship them in a package directly to the job.

And we had framing lumber shipped in random lengths to our own yard where it was precut and packaged for each plan.

For most subcontractors and for suppliers of sliding steel windows and doors, garbage disposals, ranges and ovens, roof beams, and interior doors, we selected a certain kind of company. We wanted to be their largest but not their only customer. By offering them consistent volume, we could demand and get excellent quality and service. For some of the subs, we proposed that we would pay them just enough to cover their labor and material cost on our jobs and all their overhead. This would allow them to make a larger unit profit on smaller jobs. When I noticed that job superintendents were spending much of their time at local hardware stores and coming in at the end of the day with pockets full of receipts for such items as special nails, beam hangers, and other kinds of hardware, I got them to give me a precise takeoff for each plan, purchased the material, and had it sent to the yard and packaged there for delivery to the specific house.

Soon we were building and selling in two or three subdivisions at the same time, but we could build at a faster rate than we could sell in each of them. As a consequence, we inventoried site improvements and house slabs but had one assembly line for the construction of the rest of the house. For example, we might have three 100- to 200-lot subdivisions, each with a set of model homes and a sales office. We would start building twenty-five houses in project one, the twenty-sixth house would be in two, and the fifty-first house would be in three. Of course, we varied the numbers of houses built in each one depending on the rate of sale. I called this system the "wheel." When in 1955 we expanded operations into the East Bay, Marin County, and Sacramento, we could not use the wheel and were therefore less efficient. Sales in the East Bay and Sacramento did not go very well and soon we abandoned these areas, but we continued operating in Santa Clara and San Mateo Counties, where we could use the wheel, and in Marin, even though we could not.

Marketing, Sales, and Publicity

After I returned in mid-1954 from two years in the Army, my father asked me to take charge of sales and marketing, which also included processing loans for our buyers. Like most merchant builders, we had three or four floor plans, each represented by a furnished model. The furniture was from Herman Miller or Knoll. I hired an artist friend to design signs and displays for the model homes, which were mounted and backlit in one of the garages that we finished as a sales office. We advertised in the local newspapers and installed large directional signs. Whenever we surveyed buyers about what had brought them to a site, we got the same response. The two sources were signs and word of mouth. But when we reduced or eliminated newspaper advertising, there was a noticeable falloff in traffic. Whatever we did, there were periods when traffic and sales fell off sharply. They usually but not always coincided with a recession. My father's brother, Alvin, who was one of the salespeople and an amateur comic, would characterize such a situation by declaring, "Even the people who don't intend to buy are not coming out." Dallas builder Ike Jacobs (see Chapter I) was more eloquent: "When the prospects meet on the courthouse steps and decide not to buy, there is not a Goddamn thing you can do about it. You can give the salesmen bonuses or run more ads, but it won't work. Trying to buck that trend is like pissing against a Texas gale."

Shortly after we built the first Anshen models in Sunnyvale in 1949, Eichler Homes became a national story. There were articles not only in the local newspapers but also in regional, specialized, and national magazines including *Life, Look, House Beautiful, Sunset,* and *House and Home.* We never sought the national coverage. In fact, we often placed restrictions on it because it could be very disruptive. For example, when the editor of *Look* called me to ask about doing a story, I insisted that we pick the models and the photographer. Even then, for several days, model homes were in shambles as the photographer moved the furniture for his shots. Except in *House and Home,* which was a magazine mostly for home builders, the stories were less about my father and more about the houses themselves.

Apart from satisfying egos, all the signs, mailings, ads, and even word of mouth could do is get people to the model homes. Then the task was to convert them from prospects to buyers, which was rarely easy to do, even if they came predisposed to buy an Eichler home and even when down payments were minimal. When I took over sales, I soon discovered that our salespeople, like most others, often failed to qualify prospects, to ask a few simple questions like, "Where do you live?" "Do you own your own home?" "Do you have children?" "Where do you work?" and "What kind of work do you do?" These were important for two reasons. First, most visitors to model homes came on weekends and did it for entertainment. Second, it was desirable to hone the pitch to what mattered to the prospect. I became so concerned about this that I had taping systems put in the sales offices. The salespeople knew about this, and at our weekly Monday morning meetings we listened to the tapes. At a project where we had built a community center with a nursery school, swimming pool, and playground, the salesman talked at length about these virtues and only later asked the couple how many children they had. As was sometimes the case, they did not have children and the wife could not bear any. I also discovered that almost always people would remain live prospects only for about ten days to two weeks. If they did not sign up in that period, they would buy from another builder or not buy at all. In the latter case, they might come back into the market, but usually not for several months. One of our most difficult sales problems was that people who were moving from the Midwest or the East liked the design of the houses but were apprehensive about how their parents would react to such a "radical" step. It often took a persuasive salesman to overcome this concern.

One small incident illustrates how we, like many merchant builders, adopted new practices to streamline every process. When a couple signed a contract and made a deposit, usually on weekends, they were given a loan package and asked to fill out and sign a credit application and all the other forms required except a verification, which had to be signed by their employer. The salespeople delivered the deposit check, the contract, and the loan material at the Monday morning meeting. I reviewed the package and gave it to our loan processors. Most often there was a mutuality of interest between us and the prospective buyers. Many of them were moving from out of town to take a new job, were staying in a motel, and had their furniture in transit. We were carrying finished houses, wanted to satisfy them, were always short of money, and wanted to get the deal closed. I insisted that we be able to process and close that loan by the end of week, that is, by Friday following the Monday when we got the package. I noticed, however, that we were having trouble doing this and asked one of the processors why that was so. She said, "It's hard to get the credit reports in less than four or five days."

I said, "But we have four or five days."

She said, "No, we don't because we don't order them until we have the verification of employment, which indicates that they won't cancel." I then said that the cancellation rate was at most 20 percent and asked how much a credit report cost. She said it was $5.

I said, "Okay, if you order the credit report on Monday, you can close by Friday, but by doing so we will lose an average of one dollar per sale. I had a hat in my office, got it, put it on her desk, and said, "Every time you get a package, order the credit report right away, and I'll put a dollar in this hat."

The Leader

Sales and marketing were important, but other activities were more so, such as the choice of locations, negotiations for land, the arrangement of financing for both ourselves and the customers, getting governmental approvals, negotiating with subcontractors, deciding the order in which bills would be paid, running the construction, dealing with the architects, and choosing the exact product for each project. One man, Joseph Eichler, was in charge of all of them. The construction and purchasing managers, the architects, the controller, the job superintendents, the crew foremen, and I were never in doubt about that. Even the salespeople, the loan processors, and an in-house advertising manager, who ostensibly reported to me, could not resist acting on an order from him, even if it contradicted one I had issued. No manager but me even bridled at such conduct. Ultimately, it drove me to leave the job, but not until 1963, and even then only because I was opposed to his policies.

I still look back with a mixture of amazement and admiration at the following scene in which my father was at a construction job meeting with architects, superintendents, painters, crew foremen, and subcontractors. There he was wearing a tan gabardine suit, a light blue shirt, a dark blue silk tie, matching blue socks, brown suede shoes, and a felt hat and tromping around the dirt with men in work clothes while they discussed a construction detail that one of them had drawn on a piece of scrap wood or giving the paint foreman a piece of siding that he had taken home and to which he had applied his own mixture of stain colors. I wondered then and still do now how a man who had never had the slightest experience with such matters could approach them with such ease and could gain such respect and devotion from a disparate group of men. "Where did his interest in colors come from?" I asked myself. He had a space set up at his home where on weekends he could mix standard Cabot stain colors. He brought a sample and the formula to the painting foreman on Monday, and God help the painter who did not get the mixture right. Cabot even adopted some of the colors he invented and incorporated them into their line. Buyers could choose their exterior color as long as, in his opinion, it did not clash with those on adjacent houses. Once when he was driving through a project, he saw a painter applying an exterior color of which he disapproved. He stopped the car and ordered the painter to change the color. The man replied, "But this is what the buyers want. After all, it's their house."

"No it's not," my father snapped back. "It's my house."

An incident involving Bob Anshen illustrates the respect architects had for my father. Anshen was a flamboyant man. He was short and slim but had large hands and an almost homely face. He always dressed in the same manner—a gray flannel suit, black or red knit tie, black shoes, and white socks. He and my father had periodic blowups, one of which in 1953 led to a divorce. My father then employed a southern California architect, A. Quincy Jones, a more placid person. Anshen decided to do some work for a competitor merchant builder, John

Mackay. A year or so later, as he often did, my father took me and a few other staff members to lunch and afterward to see what the competition was doing. One of our stops was at a Mackay project, where we saw Anshen and the models he had designed. Bob walked over to my father and greeted him with a big smile, but my father was outraged and said, "Look at these Goddamned houses of yours. They violate every tenet of modern architecture, the ones you insisted that I adhere to. How could you do such a thing?"

Anshen stared at my father for a few seconds, then broke out laughing and said, "But Joe, these guys don't know any better. You would never let me get away with this." Soon there was a reconciliation, and for the next ten years both Quincy and Bob designed houses for Eichler Homes.

The Atrium

Almost always today when people in the Bay Area refer to Eichler Homes, they call them the houses with the atrium. Even those who have written histories of the houses misunderstand how this came about. The incorporation of an atrium in an Eichler home was an accident. In 1957, there was a recession and it was hard to sell houses. I even fired the salesman at one Palo Alto project and sat at the model homes myself. As was often the case at such times, we had a meeting with an architect to see what we might do to improve the marketability of the houses. We had already made the houses larger and more elaborate. Now most of our models had four bedrooms and a family room, were at least 1,600 square feet, and sold for $16,000 to $18,000.

For several hours Anshen scribbled sketches of floor plan variations, none of which pleased any of us, including him. In one of them, he had wrapped the house around an interior courtyard. My father asked him what it was, and Bob said, "It's an atrium. The Romans used to build their houses with them." We reached no conclusion and he departed. At the end of the day, my father and I returned to the drafting table and scanned the sketches Anshen had left there. He asked me what I thought of the atrium plan. I said it did not move me, and it forced a very boxy front facade. Finally we both agreed that we had little to lose by adding it to three existing model homes in a Palo Alto project. When we did, it had no great appeal to buyers, but one day Quincy looked at it and said, "I think it's a great plan and I know how to fix the facade." When we asked him how, he said we should convert the two-car garage into a one-car garage and one-car carport and put a translucent glass fence at the back of the carport. In addition, he said, there should be a gabled roof instead of a flat one and the outside wall of the hall of the bedroom wing should be changed from wood to glass.

What Quincy had seen and we had all missed was the visual impact the atrium could have. We had focused on its utility as a protected garden and still did for quite a while after we had built both versions of it. But when I visited several occupants, the women especially raved about the atrium for its aesthetics. Previously our houses had not had an inviting entryway and the hall in the bedroom wing was dark. As modified by Quincy, both defects were eliminated. The front door was now in the glass fence. When you opened it, you got a surprise: a small garden past which you saw the living room and through it the rear garden. Now the hall in the bedroom wing was light and opened on the outer side to a garden. In other words, we had stumbled on an improvement that was largely aesthetic rather than practical for its use. From 1958 on, houses with atriums became the staple for Eichler Homes.

Going Public: Expansion and Diversification

The three years from the beginning of 1958 to the end of 1960 might have been a culmination, the period when Eichler Homes as a company bore the fruit of the effort begun in 1949. By 1962, external circumstances were beginning to render success more difficult to achieve. Soon four factors would make it impossible for an Eichler home to be competitive in price or to provide a key feature. First, the costs of materials like glass and concrete, which were endemic to the product, were rising sharply. Second, other builders were adapting their still conventionally constructed houses so that they offered some of the features of an Eichler home—for example, partial atriums and more glass to rear gardens. Third, building codes were changing. And fourth, air-conditioning, which was nearly impossible or at least very costly to install in an Eichler home, was coming into more demand. In other words, the basic premise upon which the company was based, a house adhering strictly to the tenets of modern architecture, which could be sold at the same price per square foot as a conventional house with equivalent features, would no longer obtain. This reality was similar to the one Bill Levitt faced at about the same time. Each man might have taken pride in what he had accomplished and retired or, if he wanted to capitalize on the misplaced mania of some national company to own a famous merchant builder, out. But neither did. Instead each sold shares in his company to the public and diversified, although the form of their diversification differed.

Eichler Homes was the first merchant builder to go public. It did so in 1959 with a tiny offering of $300,000, but soon thereafter, it raised $2 million by issuing corporate bonds. The first form of diversification was minor and done solely to gratify my father's ego. Every so often people asked us to build a custom house, modification of a standard model for their own lot, and we had refused. Now there were more such requests, most of which came from Stanford faculty. The university had been endowed by Leland Stanford with 10,000 acres in the heart of Palo Alto with a stipulation that it not be sold. In the 1950s it decided to lease land for various uses including a regional shopping center, office buildings, and lots for the senior faculty. The commercial rents were at market, but for faculty rents were purposely set low. It was a perk. When a Stanford professor said to my father, "I love your houses, but I want one on a university lot on which I get a bargain," he couldn't refuse.

Our managers of construction, contracting, and purchasing and the architects were all diverted from dealing with production. For that reason I opposed this practice, which rarely was very profitable even without properly allocating the cost of these people. It was distracting and at best marginally profitable. Sometimes the three managers involved and I would jokingly discuss methods to keep my father away from these supplicants. From time to time, when someone we were building an individual house for turned out to be a chronic complainer, my father would even tell us to shield him from such people, but like any addict, he could not resist the words, "Mr. Eichler, I just love your houses. Won't you make an exception for me?"

This indulgence was marginally disruptive, but two others were far more serious. One was geographic diversification. We had already tried this in northern California, when we expanded into Marin, the East Bay, and Sacramento. The Sacramento experience had been especially instructive. Not only did the houses not sell well, but we also had great difficulty building them because none of the local carpenters or subs were familiar with our operating style. Apparently having forgotten those realities, my father now proposed that we go even farther afield, to Orange County in southern California and even to Rockland County, New York. At least in Rockland County, he bought only four lots and optioned the others. He sent our best superintendent to build model homes. When he had great difficulty getting the models built, the project was abandoned. Much later someone asked me why my father ever tried to build in New York. I said the only reason I could imagine was that he wanted to do something close to the city in which he grew up.

The Orange County venture was a different matter. He bought 100 lots immediately. I opposed this decision for two reasons. First, southern California builders were the most competitive in the country. They could build a house that was exactly the same as one in the Bay Area for 15 percent less. We might in time have been able to match that with conventional construction, but it would be a lot harder with our houses. If we were going to take on southern California, I argued, we should do it right by sending someone there who is familiar with all our operating methods and could manage all the activities—construction, sales, purchasing, and engaging subs. I was the only person who fit that description. When my father rejected this idea out of hand, it was only the latest in a series of actions he had taken to make sure that no one, especially not I, got any credit for an important accomplishment at Eichler Homes.

The third form of diversification was even less defensible than the others and much more threatening to the very existence of the company. It required taking on two types of projects with which no one in the company had any experience or expertise. One was the construction of high-rise apartments in San Francisco; the other was buying a large parcel of land that was literally under the water in Marin County, dredging it, filling it, subdividing it into large lots, and selling them at high prices. Against my bitter opposition, he went ahead with both. He bought the land with borrowed money and built three high-rise buildings. I left the company for six months in 1963 and for two years starting in mid-1964, the first time to do some consulting for Victor Palmieri and the second to run a Ford Foundation–financed project at the UC–Berkeley City Planning School to study a new phenomenon in the United States, the building of large, fully integrated communities outside existing metropolitan area boundaries.

In 1965 and 1966, I occasionally met with my father, usually for lunch. We talked about many subjects, mainly Democratic politics, with which he had long been involved, and only occasionally about the business. Nevertheless, I knew it was going badly. One day in the summer of 1966, my mother called to tell me he had had a mild heart attack, was in the hospital, and wanted me to visit him. He had had angina for several years, but still I was stunned and went to the hospital. I had never before seen him so listless, although he did not seem to be in any pain. He asked me to "take over things at the business."

After spending a week visiting the construction sites, talking to the salespeople and rental agents, and carefully reviewing accounts and reports, I was shocked. Home sales and apartment rentals were very slow, costs on the apartments were substantially over budget, and work on the Marin land had progressed slowly and would surely cost more than the estimates. The only way the payroll was being met and a few bills were being paid was by collecting rents and not making payments on the mortgages. It was clear that the business was insolvent and there was no apparent remedy for it. When I reported these findings to my father, he expressed neither surprise nor interest. He just told me to do the best I could. Having not then had any experience in dealing with such a situation, I sought the advice of Ray Lapin, a retired mortgage banker and an old friend of my father. Ray said I should consult a top corporate lawyer who had had no former connection with my father or the company. He gave me a name, and I met with the man. I told him that the biggest single creditor was American Savings, which had provided most of our construction loans and the money for the purchase and development of the Marin site. Each of the three apartment buildings had loans from different institutions, one of which was insured by FHA. He suggested that I formulate a plan to reduce salaries and other company outlays, including those for subcontractors, as much as possible and restructure the American Savings debt. When that was done, I should arrange a meeting with American Savings and hire a bankruptcy lawyer. We would tell the lender that if he did not agree to the restructuring plan, we would put the company into a Chapter 11 bankruptcy and ask the court to order it.

There were two reasons why an out-of-court arrangement was preferable. First, bankruptcy of a borrower can cause serious regulatory difficulties for a bank or savings and loan. Second, the existence of bondholders would make the process more complicated than it otherwise would be. In our case, the problem for American Savings could be especially acute. State regulations prohibited a savings and loan lending money for the purchase or development of land, but they allowed it to allocate a small portion of its assets to buy a parcel and develop it for sale. For that reason, American had bought the Marin land, committed funds for its development, and sold Eichler Homes an option to buy it in stages at a very high fee. However, in ensuing correspondence, its managers often referred to the transaction as a "loan."

Ironically, in an earlier transaction with American Savings, I had refused to comply with the demand of one of its loan processors that we conform to their requirement that our home buyers let them write fire insurance policies as a condition of getting a loan. This too was contrary to regulations, and an American processor had then too made the demand in writing. When Taper called me to declare his intention to cancel the loan arrangement if I did not comply, I told him that if he did that, I would report his violation to the authorities. He backed down but never forgave me.

Before taking the two lawyers to a meeting I had arranged with Taper, I told my father what I proposed to do and pleaded with him not to accept the phone call from Taper that was sure to come. "He will ask me why I have come instead of you. I am going to tell him you are ill and unavailable and have given me authority to act in the best interest of the company and its shareholders. If you take his call, he will try to shame you into using whatever money you have out-side the company to pay down the debt."

As I had expected, after I explained the purpose of the meeting, the first ques-tion Taper asked was, "Where is your father? He sought these loans. He is an honorable man and surely he will see that his debts are paid." I presented the plan and pointed out what he already knew, that bankruptcy was a bad alternative not just for the Eichler family and the outside shareholders but also for him. He said he would consider the matter and get back to me. Over the next week he and/or his surrogates and I had several telephone conversations in which we negotiated details of the plan. I thought we had reached an agreement, but he called my father and talked him into disavowing the plan and sending him several hundred thousand dollars of his own money. My brief tenure had clearly ended. A few weeks later, a small-time broker of business deals told my father that he had two clients who wanted to buy the company. My father suggested that I listen to the pitch. I asked the broker if these men were aware of the dire straits of the com-pany and how much it owed to American Savings. He said that they were, that they knew and were sure that they could work with Taper, and that they had plans that would turn the company around and make it bigger and better than ever. I asked what those plans were, and he said he did not know. My father, my brother, and I owned over 85 percent of the common stock, which they proposed to by for with notes. My brother refused to take a note but agreed to take cash at a big discount. I ran background checks on the two prospective buyers, Parr and Bryson, and learned that Parr had a small insurance agency and that Bryson was a known con man. There were warrants for him outstanding in several states. I reported these findings to my father and argued that we should stop dealing with such people. Instead I proposed that we put the company into Chapter 11 bank-ruptcy and simultaneously present a workout plan to the court. The plan would provide that all creditors, except subcontractors and suppliers, reduce their debt pro rata and that the subs and suppliers exchange their debt for all or most of our stock. He and/or I would agree to run the company at reasonable salaries and get options to buy stock. I hoped that by doing this Eichler Homes could remain in business at a smaller scale and give the subs and suppliers who had been loyal to us a shot at a recovery of some, or even all, the money they otherwise would have lost by trusting us. He summarily rejected the idea and we sold our shares to Parr and Bryson for notes. A few months later, three small, unsecured creditors put the company into a Chapter 7 bankruptcy under which it was to be liquidated by a trustee.

Insofar as my father was concerned about his legacy, he may have done the right thing by selling to Parr and Bryson before there was the inevitable bankruptcy. By doing so, he allowed many people to blame them rather than him for the decline and demise of the company. I have seen many examples of this over the years, but one particularly stands out. One of Eichler Homes' regular subs was a modest-size roofing contractor named Harold Guidi. When I began to build apartment projects for the Klingbeil Company, I asked Harold to submit a bid for the roofing. He did and got the job. I was pleased because I knew that he had lost about $100,000 as a result of the bankruptcy. I assumed he blamed my father and perhaps me as well for the loss. But one day Harold said to me, "Ned, it was really a shame that your Dad sold his company to those jerks Parr and Bryson. They sure ruined a great company." I was stunned at his naïveté but chose not to disabuse him of his erroneous assumption. His view is shared by most of the people who have made a career out of publishing stories about my father. Bill Levitt accomplished the same purpose when he sold his company to ITT.

Shortly after the Eichler Homes bankruptcy, my father invested a few hundred thousand dollars in a smaller home-building company and promoted it as "Joseph Eichler Presents…." The bankruptcy trustee claimed that the Eichler name belonged to the estate and sued him, but the suit had no practical consequence. He built larger homes individually or in small tracts until he died in 1974. I knew that his new company was in trouble when he asked me to cosign a document giving him authority to borrow $125,000 he had contributed to trusts for his five grandchildren, two of whom were my sons. I said that morally I had no objection because it had been his money in the first place. But I pointed out that the trustees would be violating an IRS rule and resigned from the role. After he died, I discovered that he had lost whatever money he had outside the business in the stock market. The only remaining capital in the new company was the money it had borrowed from the children's trusts. That money was used to pay the salary for my brother. As a result, the only inheritance for my mother was her clothes, her jewelry, her car, and the house in Hillsborough in which they lived. Fortunately she sold that for $250,000, which, along with Social Security, she lived on for another eight years.

The lives of my father and Bill Levitt were parallel in several ways. First, they were both born in the first decade of the twentieth century. Second, they both had a positive impact on the thousands of families who bought their houses. Third, they both became famous and reveled in it. Fourth, they both made a lot of money. Fifth, sadly, they both stayed in the game too long and did some bad and even illegal things near the end.

I know little about Levitt's relationship to being Jewish, his personal tastes, or his political convictions, if he had any, but I know a great deal about father's opinions on these matters. He became politically active concurrently with his success at merchant building, but he had long before demonstrated his attitude toward the role of government. Its overriding purpose, he believed, was to aid people who could not take care of themselves. Otherwise, it should avoid interfering with lives or liberties. He detested phonies and scaremongers like Joe McCarthy. He was not a reflective man, but his words and often even his actions demonstrated his conviction that a Jew who inherited or earned a lot of money had two responsibilities, two ways he should use his wealth. First, he should help those in need. Second, he should cultivate himself, not simply indulge entirely in crass activities. When in his opinion someone shirked one or both of these responsibilities, he would remark with contempt, "That a Jew should act that way."

The respective accomplishments of both my father and Bill Levitt required the concurrence of three factors: a particular man in a particular place at a particular time. As is often the case, their role was a matter of chance, not of careful calculation. Their obsession with success and with achieving it did not bode well for their relationship with their sons, but that perhaps was inevitable.

3

Launching a Star: Donald
Trump and Penn Central

In every instance of a business success, there is a confluence of circumstance and the personality of a key actor. The situation that led to my involvement with Penn Central is no exception. The circumstance was the bankruptcy of the railroad company. The actor was Victor Palmieri, a forty-three-year-old Los Angeles lawyer, who fifteen years earlier had left his practice in O'Melveny &Myer, a large, prestigious law firm, to run the real estate operations of a client, the Janss family. In 1968 he became deputy director of the Kerner Commission, which was established in response to race riots in 1968, and in 1970 he founded a highly specialized firm, Victor Palmieri Company (VPCO), to handle large-scale work-outs of troubled real estate assets for fees. His first client was Great Southwest, a solvent subsidiary of the bankrupt parent, Penn Central. The first project was a group of Texas theme parks called Six Flags. The second project was the Pennsylvania Company, also a Penn Central subsidiary, which owned securities in oil and gas operations and, by far its largest asset, Arvida, a Florida real estate development company whose properties included the Boca Raton Hotel and Golf Course and thousands of acres of surrounding land.

Early in 1973, I decided to resign from my current job and called several friends to discuss what I might do next. One of them was Palmieri, whom I had known for over a decade. When I told him I was unsure about my future course next, he said, "I'm not. You're going to be my partner. A few days ago I got a contract with the trustees of Penn Central to handle the disposition of all the company's real estate not required to run the railroad. Nobody knows how many parcels it involves, but it is probably at least 9,000. The only staff I have available for the project is a lawyer, John Koskinen, a former aide to Senator Abe Ribicoff of Connecticut and my assistant at the Kerner Commission. John is a smart guy, but all he knows about real estate is the mortgage on his house. Worse yet, I have committed 80 percent of my time as CEO of the Pennsylvania Company." I told Victor that I had recently remarried and that my wife and I each had a teenage son living with us. I told him that we might be wary of moving them to D.C. "Okay," he said, "but at least do this for me. Meet with John, visit members of the Penn Central real estate department and all the Eastern and Midwest cities where it has significant, potential real estate holdings. I say 'potential' because many of these sites are yards that might generate more revenue if detached from the railroad operation and sold. Write reports about what you learn and what you think should be done." We agreed on a consulting fee, and for the next several months I performed as Victor had proposed.

During this review, I reached four conclusions: (1) that while he did not know much about real estate, John Koskinen was very smart, had an acute sense of the politics of the task, and was a fast learner; (2) that the company's real estate people would be more a hindrance than a help because they were ingrained with the concept that the only purpose of the yards and related properties was to facilitate freight operations; (3) that just getting accurate legal descriptions and conditions of title was going to be a major undertaking; and (4) that the market for commercial and residential real estate in many of the cities involved, especially New York, was deeply depressed by a combination of excess supply and a national recession. The city of New York itself was in receivership, hotel occupancies were already low and declining, and office vacancy rates were high and rising. Upon reflection, I realized that there was some light in this otherwise dark picture. In the workout business, it is better to take over assets at the bottom of the value cycle than when they are still falling. Whether that bottom had yet been reached was unclear, but surely there had already been significant decline.

My review revealed an unexpected example of Palmieri's special talent for the unusual role he had carved out for himself. John had suggested that it would be politic for me to call on Charles Seymour, partner in Jackson Cross, a Philadelphia appraisal firm which was a regular adviser to Penn Central senior management and which had itself competed for the contract Victor had obtained. When I met with this Seymour, he proudly showed me four large floors filled with his employees and then took me to lunch. As I was lifting a spoonful of soup to my mouth, he said, "I wanted the job you guys got, but, of course, we could not compete with the large, professional staff Palmieri has in Los Angeles." I barely got the soup in my mouth and swallowed it without choking. I knew that Victor's crew in Los Angeles consisted of a secretary and an administrator. Soon, however, I realized that he was exactly the right man for the job for several reasons. First, he had a quick grasp of the nature of problems and of how they might be solved. Second, he could attract high-grade people for the tasks required both because he made them partners in the fees and because, while he was sometimes brutal in his criticism, he treated them with respect. Third, he could gain the trust of many different kinds of people. Fourth, he had the knack of turning what seemed a trap into an advantage.

The last point is illustrated by an incident. The proposed contract with the Pennsylvania Company allowed Victor to put on the company's payroll senior executives of his choosing, but it also required him to spend 80 percent of his own time on its affairs. The compensation to VPCO was $300,000 per year and 5 percent of any increase in the value of the company over five years. The contract had to be approved by the federal judge presiding over the parent's bankruptcy after a hearing. In this and most large-scale bankruptcies, it is standard practice for the shareholders, however much it may appear that they have no equity, to be represented by counsel and for him or her to object to almost every act of the trustees. In this case, the shareholders' lawyer was David Berger, a particularly flamboyant advocate and a man who will appear again later in this story. Victor had arrived dressed in slacks and a sweater. John urged him to buy a suit, shirt, and tie to wear for the hearing. Victor told him to forget it, that he would be fine. When he took the stand, he apologized for informal attire. The judge chuckled and assured him it would not be held against him.

Already upset at Victor for ingratiating himself with the judge, Berger went on the attack. After citing the terms of the contract, under which Victor was to spend 80 percent of his time running the company, he asked him where he lived. The calm reply was "Malibu, California." Berger then inquired if Victor intended to move to Philadelphia. Without hesitation, Victor said, "No."

Certain that he now had the witness where he wanted him, Berger shot back, "Don't you think it would be better for the company if you did?"

He expected a lame dissertation on how Victor could still do a good job as a commuting CEO, which, of course, he was prepared to challenge. But Victor trumped him. "I suppose it would," he said, "but the trustees know where I live and approved the contract on that basis." The hearing was over and the judge soon approved the contract.

I shall have more to say about Palmieri later. Suffice it to say now that when I completed my investigation in the summer of 1973, I reconsidered my earlier refusal to accept a long-term role with his company. I had come to like and respect John Koskinen and thought he and I would make a good combination, his skills at politics and administration combined with my skills in real estate. We moved to the Washington area because that is where the VPCO headquarters was.

Not long after I started working in VPCO's Washington office, the receptionist told me that a man named Donald Trump was on the phone asking whom he should talk to about the two giant Penn Central yards on the West Side of Manhattan. I asked loudly, "Who the hell is Donald Trump?" No one answered. When I pressed the button on my phone and said, "This is Ned Eichler," a man aggressively asked, "Are you the guy I talk to about buying the West Side yards?" I said I was and he said, "Good, I want to buy them. I want you to come to Brooklyn to see the 6,000-unit, federally subsidized apartment project my father and I are building and we can talk there. When are you coming to New York?" I said I would be there on Tuesday of the following week and could probably have some time in the afternoon. He said that was fine, asked me where I would be, and said he would send a limo for me.

I have already depicted the state of the economy and the real estate market in New York at the time. Now I shall offer more detail on the two yards. Both of them were on the West Side of Manhattan, one about thirty acres at 30th Street and the other about sixty acres at 60th Street. The latter straddled the West Side Highway, with about one-third of it under the water in the Hudson River. Its location was superior to that of the smaller yard, but there were more physical and political impediments to its development. Building apartments on the submerged land would require substantial extra cost for the construction of pilings to be sunk into the riverbed and the highway would need to be relocated. To make matters worse, high-rise buildings on the site would block views of tenants in existing buildings. At the time, there was a track originating in the north, running through both yards and ending at 14th Street. Trains carried freight to one customer at 60th Street, paper to print the *New York Times*, and fourteen small businesses below 30th Street, which were the remnants of a once major produce area that had been relocated. There could be no reasonable argument for maintaining this limited service.

I understood these circumstances and also knew that every experienced, large-scale apartment builder in the city was in deep financial difficulty or at least had existing projects that were experiencing major vacancies and/or very slow rent-up. Some expressed interest in one or both sites but refused to consider anything but a rolling option under which they would make only a token initial payment and would be allowed an open-ended amount of time to get development approvals and financing. in some cases, they said they would be interested only if Penn Central advanced most of the money required for plans, engineering studies, and various other consultants. The appraised value of the two yards together was over $100 million. It became clear that the only way we could get work started on designing projects was to structure a form of joint venture under which a number of units would be agreed upon, the purchase price would be paid over time as construction was started on groups of units, and strict time limits would be set for performance. If any of these limits were not reached, the seller would have the right to cancel the transaction and get possession of all the plans. Under no circumstance would Penn Central pay any portion of the $3 million to $5 million initial outlay. In effect, therefore, our job was to identify the best horse to ride, that is, the developer who was most likely to bring the projects to fruition and who would agree to the kind of transaction cited above.

After several weeks of meetings with Trump and other prospective developers, I concluded that Trump was our best choice for the following reasons: first, he agreed to bear the risk of the initial outlays and to the principle of a specific timetable; second, he and his father had no competing projects in Manhattan and no projects in Brooklyn that were in trouble; third, he had demonstrated a thorough knowledge of the planning, financing, and construction process; and fourth, and most importantly, he was maniacally committed to using the project to establish himself as a leading New York developer. One day when we were walking in Central Park, Trump pointed to the tall buildings on Fifth Avenue and Central Park South and said, "I am twenty-nine years old. I don't drink or smoke. I am not married and will stay that way. In five years I'll be the biggest developer in this city and in ten years I'll be dead." He was like a character from a nineteenth-century French novel in which the hero leaves the provinces to conquer Paris. When people who live in one of the boroughs go to Manhattan, they say, "I went to the city," which for them is not even all of the island but only the portion south of 86th Street. Similarly, when the French talk about Paris, they mean only the city center.

By the summer of 1974, I was spending so much time in New York, dealing not only with Trump on the yards but also with prospects for several other properties, that my wife and I decided to move there and put the kids in private schools. As Trump and I were getting close to agreement on terms for a deal on the yards, I confronted him with the following problem: "I am reasonably confident that we can conclude a deal and get it approved by my partners, the trustees, and the court if I can be satisfied on one outstanding issue. How good will you be at driving these projects through the morass of the city approval process? How can I be convinced and convince the others that you are the best man for this task?"

Trump thought for a moment and replied, "I guess you should ask the mayor."

I said, "Well, I would like to do that, but I don't know him, and given his and the city's hostility to Penn Central, he won't want to talk to me."

In his typically brash way, Trump shot back, "I can get him to see you. When do you want to do it?"

"Come on, Donald," I said, "don't play games with me." He said he knew the mayor was in town and repeated his question. "Okay," I said, "if you insist on this nonsense, tomorrow afternoon."

He walked a few steps away, made a call, and said, "The limo will pick you up in front of your office at 1:30 tomorrow to take you to his office. I'll meet you there."

As I rode downtown in the limo, I remembered that the current mayor, Abe Beame, came from Brooklyn and probably knew the Trumps. When I arrived at his office and announced myself to his secretary, she said, "Go right in, Mr. Eichler. The mayor, the Trumps, and John Zuccotti [the city planning director, whom I knew] are waiting for you."

As I walked through the door, I had to stop myself from laughing at the scene. In the mammoth office, Beame, who was very short, was flanked by Donald and his father, both of whom were well over six feet tall. It might have been my imagination, but somehow the mayor got his arms around each of them. Zuccotti remained in the background. As I approached, Beame glared at me and in a clearly hostile tone asked, "What do you want?"

Taken aback, I stumbled through an explanation. "Donald and I are close to agreement on a joint venture for the Penn Central yards. I need to satisfy myself, my partners, the Penn Central trustees, and the court that he is the best choice to get the project through the difficult maze of city requirements. He thought the best way to do that might be for me to put the question to you."

Without skipping a beat, Beame said, "Whatever the Trumps want in this city, they get." In less than two minutes, the meeting was over. I thanked the mayor for seeing me and for his frankness, shook hands with Zuccotti, and turned to leave. Donald asked me to wait outside for him and his father.

This was the only time I ever met Donald's father, Fred, but as we talked after the meeting, I realized that it was a very different relationship from what I had experienced with my father or what I knew of some other father–son relationships among successful developers. Fred Trump's story is not untypical in the field. He started out building a few duplexes and shifted to small apartment buildings and then to larger ones. Over the next two or three decades he built thousands of units and kept them all. By 1973, his portfolio was over 20,000 units. In total contrast to his son, he did everything he could to stay under the radar. He was, in other words, an extremely private man. He was well aware that Donald wanted to conquer the big city and was willing that he should have a few million dollars and whatever political help his father should give him. He would not, however, pledge his assets to the pursuit, and I have no reason to believe that Donald asked for it, but it was clear that he was more than pleased to have his son get all the glory. He was at the meeting only to add weight to the proposition that Donald had strong political connections.

I kept Palmieri and Koskinen informed of the progress of my negotiations with Trump, why I had chosen him, and what happened at the meeting with the mayor. Each approached the matter with appropriate skepticism but from somewhat different angles. Victor challenged me mainly on substance. Was this the best way to go about disposing of the yards? Was there not another developer who would put up more money and/or be a better horse to ride? John was more concerned with the appearance and the politics of the transaction. Could we convince the trustees and the court that this was the way to go? Was this the right time to confront them with what to them might well seem a flaky deal? In the end they decided to proceed. The proposal was submitted to the trustees, who grudgingly approved it. At this point David Berger, the shareholders' lawyer, whom, as related earlier, Victor had bested on a different matter, reappeared.

As is true in most big bankruptcies, Penn Central's creditors were owed far more money than the company's assets were worth. Therefore, under the law, there would be no money for the shareholders. The trustees' constituents were these creditors, which in this case meant practically every big bank or insurance company in the country. The real fight was over which, if any, of these creditors was secured and, if so, by what assets and in what order. It was a paradise for bankruptcy specialists from large law firms. The task of a lawyer representing the shareholders is different. He has to throw up a smokescreen that will cause sufficient difficulty for the trustees and the court so that they will throw a bone for his clients. Furthermore, the longer he can string out the process, the higher his fee will be, a fee that is ultimately borne by the creditors. Berger was well suited for the role. He demanded that I submit myself to many hours of depositions, which were conducted by young members of his staff. It was a grueling process, but I accepted its necessity. But Trump became increasingly anxious to get the contract approved so he could get started on plans. I told him what had to happen; that there would be more than one court hearing and that Berger would do everything he could to convince the judge to withhold approval. When he asked me to predict the outcome or how long it would take, I refused to do so. At the initial hearing, Berger's performance induced the judge to agree to a second round.

A few nights later, Trump called me at my apartment. He said he had contacted Berger directly, had discussed his objections, and thought they could be satisfied. He said he had scheduled a meeting in Berger's office in Philadelphia the following afternoon for himself, me, and Hunt Dallas, the Palmieri lawyer who had worked with me on all the negotiations with Trump and who had drafted the contract. When Hunt and I walked into Berger's fancy office the next afternoon, Trump was already there. Berger then put on a performance. "I've done your job for you, and I should get part of your fee," he said. "You guys structured a contract full of holes and I dealt with Trump to fix them. Here are the changes he and I have agreed to." He then listed about a dozen alterations to the contract, which meant absolutely nothing. Hunt and I looked at each other and both knew what had happened. This was a charade. At a minimum, Berger was going to get credit for doing his job well. If Trump promised him some more tangible form of compensation, we were not going to know about it. At the next hearing, Berger made the same speech to the judge, after which, of course, he withdrew his objections and the contract was approved. Several years later a group of New York developers, including Trump, were having a dispute with suppliers of oil over the price and decided to hire a lawyer to represent them. Their choice was David Berger. It seemed quite possible this was his payoff, but I had no way of knowing that.

As it happened, over a decade later, when I had moved back to San Francisco, an investigator from the U.S. attorney's office in Brooklyn came to my house and spent over five hours interrogating me about the incident. He had read my deposition and the transcripts of the court hearings and asked me if I thought the changes agreed to by Trump and Berger improved the contract. I said that they had made no difference either way. He then referred to the contract that Berger later got and asked me if I thought it was a bribe. I told him I would tell him what I knew but not what I thought. I would not speculate. Looking back now after thirty years, my guess is that Donald told Berger he would find a way to compensate him later and did. Soon after the interview, the U.S. attorney abandoned its investigation. I am unaware of any overt crime committed by Trump. I can say that from what I knew about planning and construction approvals in New York, I would be very surprised if any successful operator could get by without paying bribes. This was one of the many reasons why I did not want Penn Central and/or VPCO even to consider trying to develop the yards or any other building project.

There were many incidents that might have led me to believe that Trump was used to paying bribes to public officials. I shall cite only two. The first was when he asked me if I would like to join him for lunch at the Four Seasons with one of his lawyers, the infamous Roy Cohn. I had lots of reasons to despise Cohn, but I was intrigued by what it would be like to meet him. Trump was late and Cohn and I were alone for about thirty minutes. He barely said a word and mostly stared into space. When Trump arrived with a flourish, he announced that he had just met with Congressman Hugh Carey, who was considering a run for governor. "He's perfect," Trump gleefully declared, "he'll do anything for money." The second occurred when we were walking down Lexington Avenue. He noticed a newspaper headline about a New Jersey mayor who had been arrested for taking a large bribe in a zoning matter. "That's ridiculous," said Trump, "I can buy a U.S. senator for much less than that." This could, of course, simply been bravado, or he could have been referring to legal campaign contributions. I had no way of telling.

I shall cite one more incident about Trump that illustrates his mania for gaining fame. In 1973, the city of New York announced plans to build a convention center on the Hudson River off 42nd Street. One day after that, I suggested to Trump that I might offer the 30th Street yard, which was not such a desirable location for apartments, to the city as an alternative. "After all," I said, "the city is broke and it would be far cheaper to build on land than on pilings in the river."

"Are you crazy?" Trump asked. "A lot of important people like the Tisch brothers have bought up land around the proposed location. They don't care how much the center will cost and neither will the mayor or any other elected officials." In fact, a few years later the city did decide that the engineering problems were so severe that building in the water was infeasible and turned to the 30th Street yard. Trump demanded and got a fee of $500,000 for "arranging the transaction" but then offered to waive it if the center carried his name. The city refused, and he took his fee.

Despite all the attention I, Palmieri, Koskinen, Berger, the trustees, and, of course, Trump himself and others paid to the yards, it was not that deal which made him. It was his purchase of the Commodore Hotel. Penn Central owned four hotels around Grand Central Station. The largest and the worst of them was the Commodore. It had over a thousand rooms, more than half of which were uninhabitable, a substantial vacancy rate even in the rooms that could be occupied, union contracts that required continued payments to workers even if, as everyone supposed, it would be closed and torn down, and an estimated $3 million cost for demolition. Furthermore, demand for hotel space in the area, even for hotels that were in far better condition than the Commodore, had almost collapsed, and it was appraised for $10 million. There had been many prospective buyers who, after learning all this, said to me, "You guys should pay me to take this turkey off your hands."

I had gone over these facts with Trump as I had with many others interested in Penn Central properties and assumed he had no further interest. But one day he walked into my office and said, "I want to buy the Commodore."

I replied, "Come on, Donald, don't waste your time and mine. You know the facts. You would have to pay $10 million cash and cover the costs for demolition and the payouts to the workers."

"I have no intention of tearing it down and I will pay the price," he said.

"What the hell are you going to do with it?" I asked. He replied that he was going to strip it down to the frame, remodel it, and reopen it as a "Grand Hyatt." He had persuaded Jay Pritzker to be a joint venture partner and to manage it as a Hyatt. I later learned that he had trapped Pritzker by registering the name "Grand Hyatt," which was sufficiently different from the name, "Hyatt," which the Pritzker family owned. I asked how much the remodeling would cost and where he was going to get the money. He said the cost would be about $75 million and that he had arranged financing with a major financial institution. He gave me names to call to check on both the Hyatt partnership and the financing. They confirmed what he had told me. My last question was about the unions.

"Don't worry about that. I'll handle them," he said. "Besides, I am going to get property tax abatement from the city for several years." As matters turned out, Trump's timing was perfect. By the time the Grand Hyatt opened, the central Manhattan hotel market had substantially recovered.

It would be a long time before he could get construction going on the 60th Street yard, but he was launched. Soon he bought the Plaza Hotel, began planning and then building Trump Tower, an office building on Fifth Avenue with luxury condos on the top floors, and buying casinos in Atlantic City. For a few years in the late 1980s and early 1990s, it appeared that he had overextended himself and might be on the verge of bankruptcy, but by 1995, he was once more on the rise. In 1997, I had retired and was living in New York, where I had undertaken an effort to help revive a wonderful program in which a woman taught violin to poor, mostly Black children in three Harlem public schools. Having heard that Trump's new wife was interested in the arts, I thought I would take a crack at getting a contribution from him. Palmieri had donated $10,000. I called Trump's office and his secretary said that he was in Moscow and was sure he would see me when he returned and that I should call back for an appointment.

When I did meet with him, he immediately started pulling out press clippings and reading segments that touted his comeback. When he seemed finished, I said I wanted to make a comment and then ask him a question. "It was inevitable that you would have a big rise, then a fall, and then a rise again. That is an old American story. What I would like to know is what, if anything, you have learned from that experience." It was clear that he had no idea what I meant, and I dropped the subject. Soon I left and have not seen or talked to him since.

4

End of an Era: William Levitt and the Trusteeship

William (Bill) Levitt differed from almost all other merchant builders in two respects. First, his family had been in home building before World War II. From 1920 onward, his father, Abraham, specialized in real estate and loaned money to building contractors for land acquisition. In 1929, he backed into the business when he took over forty lots, some with unfinished houses on them, in payment of a debt. He completed and sold the houses, decided to continue building, and created a corporation, Levitt and Sons, with twenty-two-year-old Bill as president and his younger son, seventeen-year-old Alfred, as vice president. During the 1930s they successfully built houses in exclusive neighborhoods on Long Island. When the war started and private home building was banned, the company got a contract with the Navy to build housing for shipyard workers at Norfolk, Virginia. In 1943, Bill became an officer in the Seabees.

When he left the Navy in 1945, Bill recognized that all the conditions I cited in the previous chapter were in place. Anxious to make a great deal of money, he decided to cater to a mass market, instead of the smaller, upscale customers the company had been serving before the war. Furthermore, he had had considerable experience with streamlining production both in the limited operation before the war and in the Navy housing. With the already established reputation of Levitt and Sons, and excellent timing, it was not difficult to get control of a large potato farm on Long Island. He was even helped by nature. A disease, "golden nematode," was wiping out the potato crop.

The second difference was in scale and in the use of the name. In the two decades after the war, he built four large projects in succession—the first, 6,000 homes in Long Island; the second, 17,000 in Bucks County, Pennsylvania; the third, 12,000 in Willingboro; and the fourth, 12,000 in San Juan, Puerto Rico.

Except in Puerto Rico, he built not only houses but also shopping centers and parks, schools, and other facilities, which he later turned over to the local government when it was created. There had been very large housing projects built in other parts of the country in the same period. For example, Mark Taper and two partners built 25,000 houses in a project called Lakewood in Long Beach, California. But they did not put their names on it and never built another one. In fact, in the early 1950s, Taper began to buy local California chartered savings and loan associations and within a decade merged them into one company, American Savings, which became the second-largest thrift in America.

Levitt had a big ego and created a brand insofar as the Levitt name was synonymous with very large communities for working- and lower-middle-class families. For that accomplishment, he even got his picture on the cover of *Time* magazine. Not only did he have the idea of building complete communities at low prices, but he gambled on many nontraditional features and construction methods. For example, to save time and money, he eschewed basements, instead using concrete slabs in which electric radiant heat coils were embedded, and chose a Cape Cod style, which was a one-story house with an unfinished attic. He had many of the materials precut, packaged, and delivered to each house and broke union rules and unions themselves by forcing most workers to specialize and to be paid by the piece rather than by the hour. He also employed his own salespeople and loan processors.

By as early as 1955, the tide in the continental United States was turning against Levitt. From a high of $48 million in 1954, sales volume fell. In 1958, it was only $18 million. In the years 1957 through 1959, annual company earnings were below $500,000, while in two earlier years, 1951 and 1954, they had exceeded $3 million. Certainly by the late 1950s, it was no longer possible to buy a large enough parcel of land at a low enough price to do what he had done for the first seven or eight years after the war. Furthermore, consumer demand had changed. It was more varied and not as concentrated at the low end of the market, which was increasingly being served by resales.

In the late 1950s, he began to look both to other American markets and abroad for the kind of opportunity he had found in the Northeast a decade before. He settled first on Puerto Rico.

But the situation in the Commonwealth had some inherent limitations. There was an emerging market for inexpensive houses. However, except at the high end of the market, houses in Puerto were built entirely out of concrete, a method that did not lend itself to organizational changes to reduce time and cost. In addition, there was competition from another large American builder, Centex from Dallas.

Both managed to build and sell quite a large number of houses at a decent profit, and over the next ten to fifteen years, Levitt built and sold more than 10,000 houses, but they were incurring a potential obligation to home buyers for which they made no provision. Concrete cannot be prevented from experiencing cracks over time. By the early 1970s Levitt was being barraged with customers' complaints about leaking roofs and wall cracks.

The other overseas market Levitt decided to tackle was France. After all, he asked himself, was there not a burgeoning French middle class, the members of which were just as anxious to have inexpensive suburban housing as Puerto Ricans and Americans? But there were cultural and legal impediments to achieving the economies of scale that had been the essence of his success. Nevertheless, he not only pushed ahead in these two markets but also expanded in the United States by purchasing large, but not Levittown-sized, sites in suburban Chicago and Washington, D.C., and initiating studies of many other areas. To what degree these attempts to broaden the geographic base of Levitt were motivated simply by ego and frustration or by a keen sense of another kind of marketing—that is, of stock rather than houses—is not and cannot be clear. In any event, they coincided with his decision to take his company public.

Levitt and ITT

Americans have often been addicted to fads on different subjects, especially those related to business. The 1960s were no exception. Business and even general-interest publications were replete with stories acclaiming the virtues of scientific management. Under this rubric, any activity in which a company was engaged could be made vastly more efficient by the disciplined, informed application of certain principles. The place to become fully educated about and trained in the practice of scientific management was graduate schools of business. The place to apply these skills was a conglomerate, that is, a firm that brings under its umbrella companies that offer many kinds of products and services. The self-appointed and widely acknowledged champion at this game was Harold Geneen, chairman of the International Telephone and Telegraph Company (ITT). He created a fully staffed department whose sole purpose was to analyze candidate companies and to buy those that were promising. In one year, ITT made fifty-seven corporate acquisitions in fields as disparate as car rental (Avis) and the manufacture of firefighting equipment (Grinell). In 1968, Geneen bypassed the acquisitions department and personally negotiated an exchange of ITT stock for Levitt and Sons, two-thirds of which was owned by Bill Levitt. The price in the then value of Levitt stock was $92 million. Levitt became the third-largest shareholder in

ITT and received several perks, including use of the company plane, three secretaries, and a large office in the elaborate headquarters he had just had built at Lake Success, Long Island.

Bill Levitt was sixty-two years old at the time of the merger and, like any aging founder, a difficult man for corporate executives to handle. Anticipating that this reality might make it harder to sell his company, he had hired a young lawyer, Richard Wasserman, and anointed him as his successor. As it turned out, Wasserman's own ambitions to make Levitt the first merchant builder to gain national and even international domination in the field coincided with those of Geneen and his executives. In the three years following the purchase, ITT advanced large sums of money to its newly acquired company to buy land and add staff. By 1973, Bill Levitt and Wasserman were gone and ITT had installed several of its own people in three key posts in the company, president, executive vice president, and chief financial officer.

Among the many companies ITT acquired in 1971 was Hartford Fire Insurance Company. In response, the Justice Department, which had fought and lost many battles with ITT, charged it with gaining monopoly power by its sheer size, not because this particular purchase restricted competition in the insurance industry. The parties could not reach a settlement and the suit was tried in Federal Judge Stanley Blumenfeld's court in Connecticut, the state in which Hartford Fire was domiciled. ITT lost the case and, according to a settlement reached by the parties, the judge issued an order giving ITT two choices: either dispose of Hartford Fire or sell five other companies, one of which was Levitt. ITT elected the latter and was given three years to dispose of the five companies. Any not sold by that time were to be placed in a trusteeship for sale. Three smaller companies were sold but two, Avis and Levitt, were each placed in a separate trusteeship. Avis was quickly sold, but disposing of Levitt was far more complicated.

The Trusteeship

When I joined VPCO and was dealing with Trump, I was unaware of the existence of the legal proceedings cited above. I did, however, know that ITT had bought Levitt and had at least one indication of the lack of good sense being exercised by its management. In 1970, I was executive vice president at the Klingbeil Company, a Midwest-based garden apartment builder that operated in several areas, including northern California. In that capacity, I attended a meeting of the Council of Housing Producers, an association of about twenty large-scale builders of homes and apartments. One of the attendees was Herman Sarkowski, president of United Homes, a merchant builder from Seattle. I knew that the recent troubles at Boeing had greatly harmed the economy of Seattle in general and homes sales in particular, but when I asked Herman how business was, he smiled and said, "I haven't sold a house since Boeing went to hell." Stunned at his demeanor, I asked why he seemed so happy. "Because I sold my company to Levitt for $6 million down and a $6 million earnout just before the market went to hell," he replied. I congratulated him but commented that satisfying the terms of his earnout must be impossible. "They were," he said, "but I talked Wasserman into letting me build and sell apartment projects in areas other than Seattle instead of houses to make the earnout and it worked." Later I learned that he had been able to get good prices for his apartment projects by having Levitt issue guarantees on tenant rentals for many years, a method that violated standard auditing rules.

One day in fall 1974, I was in my New York office and Victor Palmieri called me. He said that he had met a young man at a cocktail party named Larry Schaffrin, who was working for a local real estate firm. He wanted to change jobs and asked if there was a place for him in our Penn Central project. I said I did not have such a need, but Victor asked me to meet with him anyway. When I met with Schaffrin, I told him that we could hire him only if we got another project, a prospect that I thought was very unlikely in the near future. He then asked me if I knew of the legal situation at ITT and Levitt, which I described above. I said I did not. He went on to say that a trustee had not yet been appointed and that many New York investment bankers and large real estate brokerage firms were seeking the job by applying to ITT.

After Schaffrin left, I called John Koskinen in Washington and reported the conversation to him. I asked him if he knew anyone at ITT. Aware that ITT was very connected to Republicans and that not only were John and I Democrats but Victor was on Nixon's Enemies List, neither of us was hopeful, but John suggested I call Victor in L.A. Before I could contact Victor, John called back and said, "Never mind talking to Victor and never mind worrying about finding a contact at ITT. After you called, it hit me that it was likely that neither the Justice Department nor the judge would look kindly on anyone coming to them as ITT's choice. So I called a top official at Justice and told him about us. He was thrilled. He said that he was sick of hearing only about companies being recommended by ITT. He was impressed that VPCO has workout credentials, that it had been appointed by the Penn Central trustees and approved by a federal court, and that you had home-building experience. He asked me how quickly I could get a resume together and 'get over here with it.'" John was even more encouraged after he met with Justice Department officials and asked me if within a couple of weeks I could write a description of Levitt and perhaps give some indication of what the condition of the company might be. I asked if he could get me any recent financial statements, and he said, "No, just do the best you can."

From a combination of what I knew about merchant building in general, of Levitt in particular, and of what I could learn from people I knew in the business, and certain that the sharp recession which had already begun must be wreaking havoc, I drafted a twenty-five-page paper speculating that Levitt was in bad shape and difficult to sell. When we later got both Levitt's actual results and ITT's asking prices for the company, it was clear that it was always behind the curve. Within thirty days, the Justice Department informed John that they were ready to recommend VPCO to the judge and suggested that John see him. There were only two federal judges in Connecticut. Fortunately for us, Feldman, who was trying this case, had not been appointed when John was administrative assistant to Abe Ribicoff, the senator from that state. Had he been involved in Feldman's appointment, we would have been disqualified. The judge worked out a trustee compensation structure with John and told him to tell Stan Luke, the senior vice president who was in charge of the matter at ITT, that he had chosen VPCO. If Luke wanted to contest the judge's decision, he told John, he could demand a hearing. When John delivered this message, Luke was stunned but grudgingly accepted the reality.

The court order that established the Levitt trusteeship was unusual. The trustee was charged to do the following: (1) reorganize the company so that there would be a "viable Levitt" created and sold within five years; (2) divide the assets into two categories, one of which would remain in the ongoing company and the other of which would be declared wasted and sold within three years; and (3) report progress regularly to the court and ITT. The cost of the trusteeship was to borne by ITT, without limitation. I said that I thought that the monetary recovery from disposing of the assets and an operating company, or for that matter by total liquidation, would likely be far less than the current book value. This increased their apprehension that some shareholder, probably Bill Levitt, would file a derivative lawsuit against VPCO, alleging that we had taken control of a solid company worth at least book value and dissipated its assets.

As we got more information on Levitt's financial condition in late 1974, I learned that the company was in much worse shape than even I had thought, and our concerns were only heightened. Shortly after January 1, the formal date of the transfer from ITT to the trusteeship, John, I, and Julian Burke, VPCO's general counsel, went to the Levitt headquarters to meet with Gary Andlinger, a former executive at McKinsey and Company, a management consulting firm, who had replaced Wasserman. Knowing ITT's reputation for paranoia and for bugging people they distrusted, we assumed that our conversation would be recorded. After hearing Andlinger's responses to my questions, we reached a number of conclusions, one of which was that if the office was in fact bugged, he did not know or did not care.

Andlinger handed me a large folder that contained his financial projections for the next five years—in other words, the term of the trusteeship. While Julian and John were working out legal procedures with him, I took the folder to a couch at the other end of the enormous office and reviewed it. It was clear that Andlinger was thoroughly familiar with the terms of the trusteeship. He had divided the assets into two parts, an A, or ongoing, company, in which he had put $100 million of assets, and a B company in which he had put the rest. I concentrated first on the A company and looked at two items in the projections, net income and combined general expenses, which included overhead, sales, and marketing. Successful merchant builders targeted these expenses at 8 percent of sales and rarely exceeded 10 percent even in bad times. In year one there was a loss in every one of the projected metropolitan areas, and general expenses were 23 percent of sales. In the fifth year, there was a positive net income of $5 million. General expenses had fallen, but only to 14 percent. The projected loss for the B company was over $60 million.

When the discussion of legal procedures was over, I rejoined the meeting and told Andlinger of my concerns. "On your projected numbers," I said, "for the A company in which you have placed the best assets and in which there is no debt, even in year five the net income is only $5 million or a return of 5 percent on the investment. ITT could buy Treasury bonds and get a better yield than that." I went on to tell him how ridiculously high his general overhead was and my concern about the large loss in the B company.

His response was surprising and, to me at least, shocking. "What do you guys care?" he asked, and went on, "ITT is bearing the cost of it all." In a far more measured tone than I would have used, John explained that we could not approach the trusteeship so casually for two reasons: first, we had every reason to assume that we would be the target of a derivative lawsuit, and second, we were proud of VPCO's reputation for doing the best for our clients and did not intend to tarnish it at Levitt.

When we left, I told John and Julian that we should get rid of Andlinger as soon as possible. John agreed that we would have to do this at some future time but suggested keeping him around for a while. A few weeks later Andlinger made several requests to the three of us. First, after complaining about rising personal expenses, he wanted a raise in his $200,000 salary; second, he wanted a new company car; and third, he wanted to "drop in on the operation in France and then have two weeks off to ski in the Alps." Even John had then had enough and soon thereafter told him his employment at Levitt was over.

Like virtually all merchant builders, Levitt had a regional manager for each of the areas in which it operated. We decided to bring all of these managers to Lake Success and have them report on the situation in their respective regions. The most notorious of these men was Andrew Lorant from France. Headquarters employees described him as being smooth and glib, speaking several languages, and submitting outrageous expense accounts. On the night before the meetings, we had a cocktail party at the office for the managers. As soon as I arrived, Lorant rushed up to me and said he had to talk with me privately. I said it would have to wait for his presentation the next day. He insisted that it could not and begged me to take him to a private office, which I did reluctantly.

When we were alone, he said there were two vital matters we needed to discuss. The first was personal. He had had the French subsidiary write him a check for $40,000, which he had cashed and then used to bribe a French government official. The French tax authorities had discovered that he did not declare the money as income and demanded about $20,000 in back taxes. He wanted me to authorize a payment of enough money for him to cover the back taxes and the tax he would have to pay on the extra income. I was appalled and said to him, "You must be crazy. I am effectively an officer of a federal court and have to account to it and to ITT for every cent that we spend. Are you suggesting that I get you a check for about $30,000 and enter it as 'bribe'?"

He seemed genuinely surprised. "But Wasserman knew about and approved the payment," he said.

"Andrew," I asked him, "even if what you say is true, do you really expect Wasserman, who has been gone from Levitt for some time and who is a lawyer, to write me a letter and say that he had authorized your paying a bribe? And even if he were dumb enough to do it, which he is not, I still would not reimburse you."

Lorant's second issue, while less lurid, was more disturbing. He said that Levitt France owed $5 million to a French bank, Societe Generale, and was losing money even without servicing the debt. If I did not give him $1 million to take back to France, the company would have to declare bankruptcy. I asked if our client, the parent company, was legally obligated to pay the debt. He said it was not, but "everyone had always assumed that Levitt, U.S., would pay anyway." I told him that we would not act on any such assumption, that he could make his case to me, Burke, and John the next day. After we heard his story and talked to Victor about the matter, we decided that we did not have enough information to deny him the money, but that I should go to Paris as soon as possible to assess the situation.

After a review of the management at the headquarters and the regions, including the conditions of the housing market, I reached the following conclusions: first, that the company had to start shutting down operations in five regions, Detroit, New Jersey, California, Seattle, and Montreal; second, that the operations in France and Puerto Rico should be continued but required more detailed analysis as to how; third, that there should be further study of conditions in Spain, Florida, and Washington, D.C.; fourth, that Chicago was the only region which required only minor changes to be kept going; and fifth, that not only were there too many people at the headquarters, but almost all of those at the top were unsuited for the task ahead.

In the next six months we made drastic personnel cuts at the headquarters and initiated a search for new people in key positions such as chief financial officer, general counsel and national supervisors of construction, land acquisition and disposition, sales, consumer mortgages, and marketing. I became acting president, and we replaced ITT's auditor with Kenneth Leventhal and Company. By the end of the first year, we decided to continue operating in Florida but not in Washington, D.C., or Spain. Thus we had pared down the areas of continuing operations to Chicago, Puerto Rico, Florida, and France. However, except for Chicago, there still needed to be changes in management or product type, or both, in each region. Before I describe how we went about this, I shall relate some incidents that illustrate how much better the reorganization of Levitt could be done by a trustee with no vested interest in defending past actions than by ITT or its surrogate. And as a prelude to that, I shall describe my one and only encounter with Bill Levitt, whom I had never before met.

In the months leading up to our appointment, he had been making statements to reporters, who were more than willing to quote him at length without challenging his assertions. His claim was that he had handed a company in wonderful shape to ITT, a contention that I have herein dispelled, and that they had ruined it. An accurate depiction would have been that ITT bought Levitt Corporation for much more than it was worth, that it was already in decline, and that ITT made it far worse. Hoping to avoid, or at least limit, Bill Levitt's using his access to the press to bad-mouth us, John suggested that he and I pay a courtesy call on him when he was in his office at the headquarters. As we walked from one end of the building where my office was to the other where his was, I said to John, "I have never met Levitt, but I am sure my father did, and he and my father were the only two merchant builders in the 1950s who achieved national fame. That Joe Eichler's son should now be running his company, and scaling it down at that, cannot please him. I'll bet you he will try to find some remark to put me down."

When we entered his office, I saw a man smaller than I had envisioned seated in an oversized chair. He looked at me and said, "Ned, I haven't seen you since you were in knee pants." I almost clapped in acknowledgment of the brilliance of this salutation. How better could he have put me in my place?

Debt and Land Sales: Detroit, France, and Colorado

Broadly speaking, there are two categories in which a workout specialist can benefit the shareholders and/or executives of a parent company. Both stem from not having been responsible for and therefore not being defensive about previously adopted policies that have turned out to be wrong. For example, when I suggested selling certain assets at a stated price, most Levitt executives said to me, "We can't do that. That's below book value."

After a few such responses, I gathered them all together and told them how we would approach marketing an asset. "We are going to assume that we inherited the property from a grandmother, and that we don't know what, if anything, she paid for it. Our sole task is to get the maximum proceeds. We can disagree over what the current market value is and whether or not it will change in the near future, but I don't want again to hear anyone suggest that we consider book value as relevant. And, by the way, the same kind of thinking should be applied to debt. If it is secured by a parcel, the first question we should ask is whether the market value exceeds the amount of the loan. If it does not, we should take a hard look at whether we can avoid repayment or at least reduce the loss." I was so concerned about payments being made for presumed obligations without such a review of our options that I instructed the CFO that no check for more than $25,000 could be sent out without my signature.

The first test of this dictum came in relation to land in suburban Detroit, which at the time was the most depressed economy and housing market in the country. Several years earlier, Levitt had bought a very large parcel of land from Ford Motor Company's real estate subsidiary. The purchase contract was signed by a Levitt subsidiary that had no other assets—in business parlance, a shell corporation. The total land area was divided into four sections, the first of which was purchased for cash. The other three were scheduled for payment in successive years. To me and to any real estate lawyer, this was the same as a purchase of the first parcel and a series of trigger options, each of which had to be exercised at a specific date in the future. Levitt had developed and started to build on parcel one and currently had 700 unsold houses finished or under construction. I sent Jay Krinsky, a former colleague whom I had brought in to oversee land sales and acquisitions, to Detroit to ascertain whether there was any reason why we should draw down the second parcel and pay for it. He returned and said there was not. Consequently, I did what I thought was courteous. I wrote a letter to Ford telling them of our decision and offering to give them any land planning we had done for future parcels. The next day Jay came running into my office carrying a check for $1,000,000, which the CFO had signed and was about to mail to Ford. When I asked the CFO why he had acted against my specific order, he said, "I didn't think it included payments for which both Levitt and ITT are obligated." When I explained to him that a debt of a shell corporation was not such an obligation, he said, "Oh, that was just a technicality. ITT always pays what it owes."

A day or two later, a Ford executive called me to express shock at my decision and demand a meeting. I gave him the same explanation I had given the Levitt CFO, and he had the same response. I told him he could come to our office if he chose, but it would not change our position. He did come with two colleagues and made the same pitch to me and our counsel, Julian Burke. I asked if he knew what a shell corporation was and why buyers used it. He said he did. Then I asked, "If you knew that, why did you not object to its use?"

He replied, "I did and the Levitt guy told us it was just a technicality and not to worry. Levitt and ITT always paid." I sent him away and suggested that he be less trusting next time.

The second test came in France. After only one visit, I knew that we had far too many employees in relation to the amount of business we were doing and told Lorant that we had to make a major reduction. He was stunned and said that the French government would not permit it. I asked him to bring in our in-house counsel, a woman, and asked exactly what, if any, conditions would justify a substantial personnel cut (which, incidentally, was sure to include her). She and Andrew said it could be approved only if the company demonstrates that without such action, it could not continue in business. I said that that was certainly true in this case. Lorant then said, "You might be right, if there were not a rich parent who would cover the expenses until things got better." The lawyer concurred.

I said, "I want to make something absolutely clear. Levitt France is a French corporation owned by Levitt Corp, which has no legal obligation to advance money to pay any of its debts or operating losses. I was against giving you the money you requested in January and it won't happen again unless there are two major changes, one of which is a staff cut and the other of which is a restructuring of the loan by Societe Generale. I want you to explain those circumstances to the French government and apply for permission to reduce personnel, the specifics of which we shall determine while I am here." Turning to the lawyer, I said, "Based not on any judgment of your ability but only on the fact that we cannot afford you, you will be included in the layoffs, but I would like you to fulfill your fiduciary responsibility by seeing us through this crisis. We shall continue to pay your salary and standard severance for doing so. The others will have to leave almost immediately." They grudgingly agreed and we did get approval from the government.

Having successfully dealt with the first of three problems at Levitt France, I turned to the second, the 25-million-franc ($5 million) loan from Societe Generale. When I told Lorant to make an appointment for me with the appropriate officer of the bank, he became very nervous. "What are you going to talk to him about?" he asked. Surprised that he even needed to pose such a question, I told him I had to ask the bank to reduce the interest rate on the loan and, of equal or greater importance, provide us with below-market interest rate loans for home buyers (the rate on the loan to Levitt was about 14 percent as was the then rate for home loans). When he asked what I would do if the bank turned me down, I said I would consent to a foreclosure, a tactic that in the United States is called a "deed in lieu."

"Will you tell the bank that is your alternative?" he asked.

"Of course," I said. "Why the hell else would a bank even consider such a concession?"

I told Lorant that I had decided that taking him with me was counterproductive but that I would take our local lawyer, Jack Kavorkian, an American who had married a French woman and set up practice in Paris. Lorant lamely protested this decision but felt it necessary to tell me what the custom was when having such a meeting: "It should be held late in the morning and be followed by lunch at a posh Paris restaurant. The bank officer should be invited to choose the wine." I told him that this was okay with me and that he should arrange the appointment and pick the restaurant.

When Jack and I were ushered into the palatial office of the bank's senior vice president, I greeted him and in my halting French began to explain the purpose for our visit. He interrupted me and in perfect English said, "Mr. Eichler, I spent seven years in our New York office, and I think it would be better if we conducted this conversation in English."

I had prepared by hand a spreadsheet, which showed that at the pace we were then selling houses and the rate on our loan, by the time we had sold and built out all the houses in our one project in suburban Paris, there would be no money left after we paid the interest on the debt and overhead and construction costs. In other words, the original principal of the loan would remain and there would be no security for it. I handed him this document and said, "This is what I came to talk to you about."

The bank officer studied the paper, frowned, and said, "This is very bad. What do you propose to do about it?"

I replied, "As you know, there is a general recession in France and interest rates are very high. You cannot do anything about the recession, but you can cut the rate on our loan and provide us with below-market rates for home buyers."

"What rate do you have in mind?" he asked.

I said, "Eight percent for each." I had anticipated a negotiation, but he just asked me what I would do if he refused. I said I would turn the company over to the bank and not force it to go through the expense and trouble of taking legal action to foreclose.

After a brief silence, he looked at me and said, "Well, we surely don't want to be in the home-building business. I guess we'll have to do as you ask. So have your lawyer draft the agreement you desire, but I have one request. Would you have the parent in New York guarantee the loan?" I said I would not. Then he asked if I would submit his request to the board with my recommendation for approval. Again I said I would not.

After that, he asked if there were any conditions under which I would recommend approval. I said, "There probably are, but they would have to be so favorable that there would be no chance we would ever have to pay, and you would never agree to them." Finally he asked if I would submit the matter to the board even without a recommendation for approval. I knew that he was desperately looking for cover and agreed to do that, knowing it would be rejected.

These discussions had consumed far less time than I had anticipated. It was now only 11:30 AM. I decided there was no point in hanging around in his office, so I said, "Why don't Jack and I go out for a coffee, start drafting an agreement, and meet you at the restaurant for lunch at the time we agreed upon, one o'clock."

He said, "Mr. Eichler, I appreciate the invitation and I would like to have lunch with you, but I am very busy. So why don't we do it another time." With that, we left. I called him several times later when I was going to Paris and invited him to lunch. Each time he politely claimed he was too busy.

As it happened, over the next year economic conditions in France improved, interest rates fell, and our houses sold faster than I had projected. The bank had not lost much by making the deal with us. I fired Lorant and temporarily put a young friend of Victor, Peter Lehman, who was living in France, in his place while I searched for a permanent regional manager. It was difficult enough to find someone suited for this role in the United States; for France it would be even harder. Any candidate had to know the business, be truthful to his boss, be aggressive without being overbearing, and understand both marketing and sales. He also would have to resist the temptation to go into business for himself. In France he also had to have a feel for the culture and know how to deal with government authorities. After a fruitless search for such a manager, I reluctantly decided to detach the French operation from the ongoing company and put it up for sale. I assumed that the buyer would be French. What I did not assume is what really happened.

Our controller in France, a thirty-one-year-old Moroccan Jew, who had come with his family to Paris as a child, worked for Arthur Anderson, and then joined Levitt, was the only executive I had retained. One day while I was in the Paris office, he asked to meet with me and said that his uncle had sold a very profitable sporting goods business and was looking for investments. He went on to say that he had proposed to other Levitt France employees that they raise a modest amount of capital, have his uncle commit a larger sum, and buy the company. I asked him three questions: first, did he know that the asking price was $6 million; second, would he seek bank financing; and third, who was going to run the company. His answers were succinct: yes, he knew the price and the group was willing to pay it; yes, they wanted bank financing and had already arranged for it; and third, he was going to run it. I asked who was providing the outside financing, and he said, "Societe Generale." As far as I know, the company did very well.

This result was an example not only of how much VPCO benefited ITT but also of a truth about merchant building. Most often, the best operators in the field have been owners who run the company, especially in foreign countries. We had already acted on this principle in Spain, where by local law an outside owner had to have a Spanish partner. When we first took over Levitt, I was told that the Spanish partner refused to sign an annual report, which every company was required to submit to the national government. A few weeks later I went to Madrid to look over the operation, which was small, and meet the partner, who had been depicted by Levitt executives in New York as crazy. In an eminently reasonable manner, the partner explained the problem. In Spain there was a large real estate transfer tax, most of which everyone avoided by recording the purchase price at 10 percent of its actual amount and collecting the rest on the side. ITT had refused to permit Levitt to do this because it would violate SEC rules. The only solution to this was to sell to a local owner. The obvious candidate was the man who already owned half the company, and he bought the rest.

The third example of our successfully limiting exposure to debt was in Colorado. Levitt's Seattle subsidiary, United Homes, was building rental projects, managing the original rent-up, and then selling them to investors (see Chapter II). One of these projects was having so much difficulty getting rented that its market price was less than the amount of the debt. I had been told that there was no clause in the loan that prevented the lender from looking to the owner if a sale of the property would not cover the debt (in legal terminology, an exculpatory clause). Julian Burke suggested that he look carefully at the loan documents to see if they had any flaw that might at least give us any bargaining leverage. To his amazement and mine, he found that the document was improperly drafted and that the lender could look only to the property. I suggested that he so inform the lender, Union Bank of Los Angeles, and tell them we would be glad to give them the deed in return for a release. Soon after he did that, Victor got a call from the president of the bank, whom he knew, and who said he was sure that VPCO was not going to use a drafting error to relieve Levitt of an obligation. Victor expressed sympathy but said it was our fiduciary responsibility to do just that.

Puerto Rico

Levitt had been building in Puerto Rico since 1963, mostly in a large project in San Juan, which was called Levittown. When we took over, we were confronted with four different problems. The first was legal and political. As indicated earlier, the standard construction method for anything but expensive dwellings was reinforced concrete for both roofs and outside walls. Inevitably the concrete developed hairline cracks after a few years. While these cracks did not interfere with the integrity of the structure, they caused roofs to leak in heavy rainstorms. These roof cracks could be quite easily repaired by patching every five to seven years. The wall cracks were only a matter of aesthetics. In the late 1960s, a few homeowners sued Levitt for these conditions and sought not just free repairs but compensatory damages for pain and suffering. Soon thereafter, a lawyer moved into Levittown and began soliciting clients for a class action lawsuit. By the time we took over in 1975, these suits had reached the Puerto Rico Supreme Court, which ruled that a builder was responsible for repairs to certain kinds of defects, of which the cracks were one, for seven years after occupancy and for repairs to the cracks for fifteen years after they were performed. Since cracks occurred about every seven years, there would no end to the builder's responsibility. In addition, the court awarded money damages.

I initiated a search for any material, such as a plastic coating, that could be used to cover the roofs to prevent this problem in the future, but none was available. Our only recourse was to persuade the Commonwealth government to enact a law limiting our and other builders' damages. The governor and several legislators knew about the situation. I held several meetings with them to urge quick action and to help them design a less punitive remedy. Ultimately they did act. The compensatory damages were eliminated, but the responsibility to make those repairs in the future was not. As result, if the operation in Puerto Rico was continued and was included in the ongoing company, a buyer would be responsible for repairs to the houses already built in perpetuity. We decided that that was a condition we could not impose on a buyer because it could not be quantified and told ITT that it would have to perform the repairs beyond the life of the trusteeship and assure any buyer of the ongoing company that this would be done.

The second problem was with the type of land Levitt had recently bought. The former management had made the erroneous assumption that there was a major market for high-rise condominiums and had purchased land for that purpose, most of which was under water and unsuited for use as a standard subdivision. A few such projects had already been built and had sold badly. The cost per square foot to build such structures, especially if the land was submerged, was far higher than it would be for standard low-rise buildings. Most people who could pay the required price preferred to buy a detached house in an upscale location where they could get a far better dwelling for less money. Thus, the land bought for high-rise units had little or no value, and its cost would have to be written down nearly to zero.

The third problem was management. The current regional manager, an American, had already indicated his desire to leave the area. I thought this was just as well because the company would be better served by having a local man for the job. I asked Levitt's executive vice president, a former manager of Latin American operations for ITT, to conduct a search and find two or three candidates for me to interview. After a month or so he said that he had found two men who might be appropriate. Both had worked in construction in San Juan, both lived there, and both had been educated in the United States, one attending engineering school and the other getting an MBA from Harvard. The former was a native and the latter was a Cuban, whose family had fled when Castro took over. I was somewhat surprised that the executive favored the Cuban. I was predisposed against him for two reasons. First, I had spent enough time in Puerto Rico to know that most local businessmen and politicians disliked Cubans. Whatever the justification or lack of it, they were viewed as interlopers, in much the same light as Blacks in L.A. viewed Koreans. I thought someone who had been a manager in Latin America would be sensitive to this issue. Second, having taught in two graduate schools of business, UC–Berkeley and Stanford, I thought it unlikely that a young man with an MBA from Harvard was suited to run a local merchant building operation. The interviews confirmed my assumption and we hired Rafael Torrens, who has successfully managed Levitt operations in Puerto Rico ever since.

The fourth, and in some respects the most serious, problem was product type. Like two other builders of large developments and several smaller operators, Levitt's houses were targeted to the low end of the market and sold for $30,000 to $35,000. It was clear that most of the pent-up demand in this price range had been satisfied and that there was too much product chasing too few potential buyers. At the other end of the market, houses for the upper middle class selling above $65,000, the scale was too limited and there was equilibrium. What did not exist was product priced at $40,000 to $60,000 and designed to appeal to an emerging middle class. How much demand there was for this and exactly what kind of house would satisfy it could be tested only by designing the product type, building model homes, and presenting them. This was the same market Levitt and its competitors were then serving in Chicago and Washington, D.C., but with ersatz colonial designs. I decided that we should try product more suited to the tropical climate in San Juan, and, incidentally, to capitalize on my experience with the more contemporary designs of Eichler Homes (see the next chapter). This meant houses that were both somewhat larger and better equipped than those we were building and more oriented to rear yards with sliding glass doors and perimeter fencing. When we built four new models and offered them for sale, they were an instant success, and Levitt established a reputation for building excellent product for this growing market.

Meetings with ITT

The court order required us to meet with ITT monthly. John and I always attended these meetings and on occasions were joined by Julian and once by Victor. The ITT side always was led by Stan Luke (see Chapter I) and usually included several other company executives. Even before the first meeting, I learned that many members of the Levitt staff had very generous severance arrangements. Contrary to my expectation, Luke and his associates were rarely interested in our accounts of the present state of Levitt's business or in what our plans were for its future. The two matters that did get their attention were the fate of former ITT personnel who had been transferred to Levitt and anything that bothered Geneen. On the former they asked us to give them notice when we intended to fire any of "their" people so that they could decide if they would put them back on the ITT payroll. When on later occasion we entered the space outside the meeting room, we saw several such people occupying desks and apparently having nothing to do.

There were two subjects in particular that caused Geneen to blow up at Luke and his subordinates. The first and most persistent was the constant flow of statements Bill Levitt was making to the press. His favorite claim was that he had "sold a great company to ITT and Geneen had ruined it." Of course, Levitt and Sons was already in decline when ITT bought it, but Geneen could hardly offer that as a defense. Whatever Luke or he believed, however, there was no question that under their leadership its decline was greatly accelerated. It was not clear that we had any legal right to prevent Bill Levitt from bad-mouthing Geneen to the press, but, under an agreement he had signed when ITT bought his company, we did have the right to try to stop him from going into business in any area where we were or might be doing business and using his name to advertise it. When he violated that provision by initiating a retirement project in Florida and promoting it in ads and press releases as "William Levitt presents...," we sued him in federal court and got an injunction. As a practical matter, however, it was very difficult enforce the order. Ultimately the court awarded damages and Bill Levitt appealed and lost the appeal, but long after the trusteeship was over and an ongoing company was sold, he continued desperate attempts to get back into business and use his name in the process.

A Nickel a Share

There was one way in which Harold Geneen's displeasure had a positive consequence for us and perhaps for ITT. As the first year of the trusteeship, 1975, was coming to an end, we had to prepare an audited financial statement for Levitt Corp. As its president, I had to sign off not only on the validity of the income and expenses calculations, which I was more than willing to do, but also on the values of the assets and liabilities that we had declared wasted. My initial decision was to tell Leventhal, the company's auditor, that for assets such as land in Puerto Rico that was under water and in Washington, D.C., or for the liability for failures to concrete in Puerto Rico, I could make only a wild guess. But Leventhal's president, Stan Ross, John, and Burke insisted that I do just that—make a guess. When I finally did that and they gave the year-end numbers to ITT's auditor, Arthur Anderson, Luke was livid.

ITT had accounted for Levitt assets and liabilities that they were required to sell by putting them in one basket of "discontinued operations." Each year ITT's management gave the auditor an estimated net value of this basket and it was entered as a "below the line" item on the financial statement. We had informed Luke and his crew about the problems cited above but had not quantified their financial effect. By the time we did that, Geneen had publicly estimated ITT's 1975 earnings. Apparently someone had made up a number for Levitt. Luke was so terrified of telling his boss what had happened that he pleaded with John to find a solution. He said that otherwise he would have to inform Geneen that his earnings estimate was off by a nickel a share. Out of a meeting between the two of them an idea arose. Insurance companies are allowed to place assets in a category called "held for long-term investment" and to value them at cost. Luke asked John if he would approve a transfer of all these questionable assets to Hartford Fire.

When John told me about the suggestion, my first reaction was that it was a sham, which it was. But upon reflection I realized that it was not our sham and that it could benefit us in two ways. First, it would marginally increase our incentive fee. More importantly, it would relieve me of having to cope with the serious difficulty of marketing these assets. John decided to try out the idea on the Justice Department. Their response was that they had no interest in helping ITT, but if we believed it was better for the trusteeship, they would not oppose it.

The Sale

In the fall of 1977, we put the newly structured and named company, Levitt Corporation, on the market through Merrill Lynch. I arranged bank financing for myself and made a bid but withdrew it because of the appearance of a conflict of interest. As far as I know, there were only two real prospects. One was Kaufman and Broad (now KB Homes), a publicly traded merchant builder operating in many areas, including France, which never made an offer. The other was Henry Benach, chairman of Starrett Housing Company, whose stock, while closely held, was also publicly traded. At the time, Starrett had three lines of business: general contracting, construction and management of subsidized rental housing, and building and selling condominiums in Iran. Not knowing that I had already withdrawn my bid, Benach called on me. He said that he wanted to diversify further, that neither he nor anyone else in his organization had any experience in merchant building and that he would make an offer for Levitt only if I and my top executives would manage it for Starrett.

I was conflicted about the proposal. On the one hand, I wanted to see how well we could do with the operation we had designed. On the other, I was wary of working for Benach. I knew the head of his general contracting division, who warned me about Benach's outbursts of anger and stubbornness. Jay Krinsky had checked on him and found that that was his reputation. In the end, I took a gamble. Benach had poured much of his company's money into a giant condo project at high prices in a suburb of Teheran and was spending most of his time on the construction, marketing, and politics of this venture. Advance sales had been very strong. If this continued, I thought, he would be so involved with this matter and making so much money at it that he would have neither the time nor the inclination to pay much attention to our less glamorous operation. With the agreement of me and my staff to manage it, in January 1978, Starrett bought Levitt Corp for $38 million, about seven times after-tax earnings. A few months later the Iranian Revolution ruined his plans and mine.

Instead of Levitt being low on Benach's attention scale, it suddenly became everything to him. It was now the most important generator of sales, profits, and cash for Starrett. In 1977, Levitt earned about $8 million in pretax earnings and Starrett took $11 million from it. Even worse, he began to micromanage the operation. For example, even though I had made it clear to him that I would not move to Florida, he ordered me to transfer the headquarters there. In addition, when I suggested that the Chicago-area housing market was about to implode and indicated my intention to sell all our land there and shift the operation to Texas, he countermanded me. He had checked with a cousin who was building in Chicago and who said I was wrong. By early 1979, a sharp downturn in home sales and land values began and continued for several years. I was right on my prediction on the Chicago market but wrong when I counted on Benach's distraction. In June of that year, I resigned and returned to San Francisco.

In the twenty-five years after I left Levitt Corp, the company went through several iterations. Starrett took it public and then sold it to a bank, which later again took it public. It abandoned operations in Chicago and cooperated with the management in Puerto Rico in selling the business there to local investors. Benach replaced me with Elliott Weiner, the controller whom I hired in 1975, and who has remained Levitt's president through all its turmoil over the last twenty-five years.

For Elliott, therefore, an association with Levitt during and after the trusteeship has been one of the few, perhaps the only, entirely successful experiences. For me it was mixed, but for Bill Levitt it was a tragedy, albeit one of his own making. In 1960, when he was completing the third "new town" in the Northeast, he might have either retired or built a large project on the east coast of Florida aimed at the same social class as the young families he had catered to for fifteen years, but a different age group, retirees. But someone else did this in West Palm Beach in two large communities called Century Village. The buyers there were people at or near retirement from New Jersey and the New York City boroughs, many of them Jews and Italians and many of them even parents of his original home buyers. Later they too would have been customers. Instead he built another Levittown in Puerto Rico, with the problems there I have described.

He got another chance to retire in 1968, this time with a lot of money, when ITT was foolhardy enough not only to pay him far more than his company was worth but also to relieve him of the burden of struggling with the many intractable problems depicted previously. He could even have gotten away with the erroneous claim that he had sold this wonderful company to ITT, who then ruined it. Few journalists would have taken the trouble to discover and report the truth. Instead, he spent the last eighteen years of his life causing great trouble and monetary loss to himself and prospective home and lot buyers of his chimerical projects in Florida. Even worse, he was sued and investigated for crimes and died broke. He was an extreme example of a common story, a once very successful and famous person who cannot face the reality that circumstances and tastes change and that advancing age limits one's ability to perform.

5

A Study in Contradiction: Larry Weinberg

When I first considered writing this book, I thought of Larry Weinberg and his life in positive and simple terms. In contrast to Trump, my father, and Bill Levitt, he was to be the man who knew exactly what he wanted to achieve as a merchant builder. He would construct a very successful company, make a great deal of money, and remain an intensely private person. He had not intended to sell out, but when national, public companies in unrelated businesses were willing to buy his company for far more than it was worth, he would, I had assumed, make plans for much greater expansion than he otherwise considered prudent to sell to, or to merge with, the highest bidder. He would agree to a down payment and an earnout, do his best to meet its terms, turn the management of the company over to others, move on to other activities like the basketball team and AIPAC, and never look back with any regrets. The only gap in this portrayal was whether he was still living and what his family life was. After completing drafts of the first three chapters, I e-mailed AIPAC to ask if he was still alive and, if so, to get his current address and/or telephone number. If he had died, I said, I would like to contact his widow and/or children. A few days later, I answered a telephone call and a voice said, "This is Larry Weinberg and I am still alive. What do you want to talk to me about?" We then had a very long conversation, which entirely altered my concept of his character. It was far more complex and contradictory than I had imagined.

Prior to this discussion, I had had three encounters with Larry, two in the early 1960s and one in 1980, when I was conducting interviews with several merchant builders in preparation for writing a book on this subject. I may have first met him when Governor Pat Brown appointed me chairman of a commission to make recommendations for ambitious new state and federal programs to solve currently perceived problems in housing. In that role, I helped the governor select the other members of the commission and traveled the state to conduct hearings with interested parties, some of whom were home builders. It is probable that in doing so, I met Larry, but I do not now recall the circumstance. The first encounter came at his request. He called to ask if he could talk to me about my father. We met and he had two questions. First, "Why does a man who is so good at organization and marketing make life so hard for himself by building such modern houses? My purpose is to have designs that are both appealing and easy and cost-effective to build. Your father insists on designs which have the opposite character." Second, "Why do you sell to Blacks and how do you do it?"

These were not illogical questions, but no one had ever put them to me. They demonstrated that, unlike other builders, Larry was concerned about his and their practice of discriminating by race when they sold houses. My answers to both questions were related. I said that his central purpose, which I did not condemn, was making as much money as possible building and selling houses of good value. By contrast, while my father wanted to make enough money to stay in business and to live well, he had an overriding objective. It was to do it by offering houses that adhered to the principles of modern architecture. Selling to Blacks was desirable but secondary. If he had believed that doing it would prevent him from achieving his main objective, he would not have tried it. I added that it was far easier for us to get away with selling to Blacks than it would be for him. Our price range was higher than his, there was more tolerance in the Bay Area than in Los Angeles, and, more importantly, the kinds of people who bought our houses tended to be more open to integration. I had gotten the feeling that Larry was asking me if our experience would provide some clue as to how he could alter his current policy. Unfortunately I could not. "Look," I said, "I am not going to tell you that the differences in our circumstances justify your not selling to Blacks, nor, on the other hand, will I say you should ignore them and do it. I can say that I for one will not disapprove of your not doing so."

My second encounter with Larry was in 1963, when I had moved to West Los Angeles to do a consulting job for Victor Palmieri. One evening my wife and I went out to dinner with him and his wife. After the meal, when we were walking on Rodeo Drive in Beverly Hills, the wives were quite a ways behind us window-shopping, and no one else was in earshot, Larry leaned over and almost whispered something to me. I don't remember the exact content, but I do know that I found what he said innocuous and of no possible interest to anyone else. Reflecting on this incident, I decided that he had an extreme penchant for privacy, a trait, for good or ill, I do not share.

My third encounter was in one of a number of interviews I conducted with merchant builders in 1980 in preparation for writing a book on the subject for MIT Press. As with Larry, I had known most of them but had not asked how they got started in the business. Larry was one of the few who had sold to or merged with a large national company. The information about him on these matters, which appears in Chapter II of this book, came from that interview. As noted in that chapter, I had assumed that Larry constructed an expansion plan for two reasons, to sell his company for a lot more money than he thought it was worth. That certainly was the view of those in and around the business at the time. I did not suggest then, nor do I now, that there is anything wrong with doing this. Even if he could have borrowed the money for such an expansion, which is unlikely, it would have been foolhardy for Larry to commit what must have been by then his considerable net worth on such an untested proposition. I was sure that he had done his best to make a success of the expanded operation, but I also noted that he had taken the reasonable step of securing a nest egg and transferring much of the risk to a buyer who could better afford to take it. I also noted in my book that before merging with CNA, he had had extensive negotiations with CBS. I had been told that by CBS founder and chairman William Paley, who said he backed away from the deal because the risk for CBS was too great.

My fourth and last encounter with Larry occurred while I was writing this book. As I wrote in Chapter II, I knew that he had left Larwin and CNA in the mid-1970s, that he had bought the Portland Trail Blazers and become very involved not only in its welfare but also in the welfare of the NBA league, and that he had been an active supporter and chairman of AIPAC, the lobbying arm of the American Jewish Committee, an organization created to promote favorable relations bewteen Isreal and the United States. I gave him a few facts about my life since we had last met, said that I was working on this book, and told him I knew that he had sold Larwin in 1969. He erupted at the last statement. "I did not sell Larwin, I *merged* it," he said.

I replied, "I knew it had been a merger, but I also knew that you left soon after you made the earnout and got $200 million in the then value of CNA stock. I assumed that you had met your obligations, sold your stock, and gone on with your life."

"That's what happened," he said, "but I didn't want it that way. I chose CNA because an insurance company could provide me with the patient capital to build a General Motors of housing." When I asked him what he meant by that, he said, "We would have an operation in every metropolitan area building housing for sale, apartments for rent, and shopping centers. And that's not all. In every region I wanted us to have a store selling all the stuff people need for their first home. We could have undersold Kmart." Weinberg contended that accomplishing all this would not only be good business, but would improve the lives of young families with limited financial resources.

I was stunned at this reply. It did not square with my view of his intentions. I then asked what had prevented him from carrying out this plan. "Two things," he said. "First, the CEO at CNA was in total sync with it, but I did not anticipate that he would soon retire. As the largest shareholder in the company, I tried to replace him with someone who would also be supportive, but I failed. The outside directors wanted a guy who would take the company in a different direction. I was outvoted seven to six. The second reason was very high interest rates, which I had not anticipated."

I told him that I did not share his view that such a plan could have worked even under ideal conditions because it required finding and handling too many exceptional regional managers. "However," I asked, "if you felt so strongly that I am wrong, why didn't you try doing it later when conditions were more favorable, and why has no one done it since?"

He said, "I had moved on by then, and I guess no one else wanted to try it." When I mentioned that in one of our earlier meetings he had asked me about Eichler Homes' policy of selling to Blacks, he immediately deflected the conversation to his own efforts at promoting racial integration in housing. He said he had called a meeting of the major home builders in the Los Angeles area and proposed that, without any public announcement, they all agree to instruct their salespeople to sell to any qualified Blacks and not to bad-mouth any of their competitors for doing so. According to him, they all refused, and one of them "came up to me after the meeting and called me a nigger lover. I punched him in the nose." He went on to say that he had become very friendly with Hubert Humphrey in 1968 and told him the federal government could do much good by changing its housing policies. He said Humphrey replied by asking him if he would accept the post of secretary of HUD, if the then vice president were elected president. Larry said he would have to think about it.

I then changed the subject to my original reason for wanting to talk to him and asked about his family. He first focused on his mother. "She was a very moral person. She had been a Hebrew teacher, and when I told her I was going to go into business, she was upset. I told her that one could do good in business and that was my ambition." Then I asked how many children he had, what they were doing, and what his relationship was with them. He said that he had four children, two boys and two girls, and that one of the boys was a psychiatrist and the other three were in the building business. One daughter and the other brother were partners and the other daughter was on her own. As he described these development activities, he used the word *we*. I pointed that out to him and asked if he was involved with them. He said, "In a way." He went on to tell me that although each of them was different, he loved and was on very good terms with all of them.

At this point in the conversation, an idea hit me. "You know, Larry," I said, "the combination of the retirement of the CNA CEO and of the high interest rates may have been a blessing for you and for your family. In order for your plan to have any chance of succeeding, you would have had to pour yourself into its execution far more than you did even to get Larwin going at the outset. As a consequence, you would have had no time to devote to the basketball team and league, to AIPAC, or to your wife and children." Larry agreed that I was right about AIPAC and basketball, but not about his family. On the latter point we agreed to disagree.

My conclusion about Larry Weinberg is that by and large he has lived an admirable life. If he has a fault, it is a very human, perhaps a particularly Jewish one. He was born with talents at conducting business, at managing a sports team, at chairing an important political organization, and at being a good father and husband. But he was never quite satisfied with these accomplishments. No doubt influenced by his mother's example and her words, he infused every activity with the burden of serving a high moral purpose. Enjoying being very good at so many varied activities for its own sake has been a difficult concept for him to embrace, but, for me at least, it is an admirable trait. Few, if any, merchant builders would even be bothered by the issue.

6

Race

It is unlikely that any merchant builder seriously considered selling a house to a Black family until at the earliest the late 1950s, except one: Eichler Homes. The question may from time to time have been put to them by a reporter. If that happened, they either refused to answer or responded as Bill Levitt did when he said that by doing so he would have seriously alienated most of his buyers and failed at his objective of providing large numbers of homes at a price that first-time buyers could afford. While I was away in the U.S. Army in 1953, my father sold a house in a Palo Alto project to a Chinese doctor, a former Olympic diving champion, and received considerable flak from the other buyers. There was one company formed specifically to build integrated housing, but its few projects were small and scattered.

As indicated in the previous chapter, in June 1954, I returned from the service and took over the management of sales, marketing, and loan processing for the company. I learned that my father had acceded to the request of Franklin Williams, the then Director of Western States for the NAACP, to buy a single lot outside any of his projects to build an Eichler home for him. It was my understanding that Frank did not want to use his friendship with my father or his position to get him to sell him a house in a standard subdivision. In my view, whatever our motivation, it would have been wrong to do it. No one would have believed that Frank's purpose was personal and not primarily political. In the fall of that year, we were building a 240-lot project in two phases in Palo Alto, named Greenmeadows, in which for the first time we were offering homes with four bedrooms. Also as a first, we had incorporated a community facility with a swimming pool, playgrounds, and a building that could be used both for meetings and as a nursery school. The price range was $16,000 to $18,000, about $2,000 on average higher than in our last tract in the area. We were apprehensive about how well these houses would sell, but our fears were unfounded. Sales went very well, and in the spring we opened for sale and started to build the last sixty units at increased prices. I was married in the same year, and my wife and I bought and occupied one of these houses.

One night I was working at our office, and the phone rang. I answered it, and a woman asked, "Do you sell houses to Negroes?" It was a subject to which I had given little thought.

Suspecting that this might be a "plant" by a civil rights organization, I asked warily, "Why do you ask?" She said that she, a nurse, and her husband, an engineer, were renting near Greenmeadows, had visited it, liked one of the models, and wished to buy one of them. Something in the way she said this convinced me that this was a sincere, personal inquiry. I told her that, as far as I knew, the matter had never come up for us before, but that I would at least like to meet with her and her husband. She agreed and invited me to come to her house. I accepted. Her husband was a very quiet, unassuming, and educated man in his late thirties or early forties. She was quite aggressive, not about the race issue but about changes she wanted us to make to the house they had selected, which was then under construction. They had no children and said there was no prospect of their having any. I got the impression that she had a medical condition that precluded conception. She worked at a nearby hospital and he at a local facility of a large corporation. I ended the interview by telling them I would discuss the matter with my father immediately in order not to keep them in suspense.

I went straight from their house to my father's and told him what had happened. He had two questions: Was the couple a plant and, if not, what did I think we should do? I said I was sure they were not a plant and continued, "Someday we are going to have to do this, both because it is right and because the government will force us to. It would be hard to imagine a better couple for our first effort at breaking the race barrier." I had been surprised at how casually he was treating the issue.

He thought for a few moments and said, "Okay, if you think we should do this, let's go ahead." We spent about an hour on unrelated business matters and I left.

The next evening I called the wife and told her of our decision to sell the home to them but rejected most of the changes she wanted. She started to argue with me about the latter, and I interrupted her. "Look," I said, "we're going to get some flak from Greenmeadows owners, and I want to be able to tell them that our policy is to sell to any qualified buyers, whatever their race or ethnicity, and that we treat them just like anyone else. I have no intention of giving you preferential treatment."

Her husband, who was on another line, interrupted and said very gently, "Dear, I think Mr. Eichler is right. We don't want to give him any extra trouble. We just want to live in one of his nice houses."

I later took their deposit and loan application and introduced them to the project salesman, after I had told him and the other salespeople about our decision. I said that selling without discrimination would be our policy from now on, that we would not seek any publicity for it, but neither would I continue to employ anyone who was opposed to it. One man said he was and walked out. In the following weeks, I worked out the precise rules we would adopt to implement the policy. It would be based on the principle that we did not discriminate in the sale of our houses by race. We operate on the assumption that our doing this did not matter to a non-Black prospect unless he asked. The specifics were as follows: (1) I would approach all the local civil rights organizations and tell them that we wanted no acclaim or publicity on this; (2) we would always answer a question honestly but would interpret the question narrowly; (3) we would not bring the matter up unless asked about it by a prospective purchaser; (4) if someone asks if we sell to Blacks or Negroes, the answer would be, "We sell to anyone who is qualified"; (5) if he asks if we have sold to a Black, the answer would be yes; (6) if he asks whether there is one in the project he is considering, the answer would be yes or no depending on which is accurate; (7) if the answer is yes and he asks how many, the answer will be the actual number; (8) if he asks where each of them has bought, he will be given the answer accurately. In other words, we were going to assume that no non-Black prospect was interested in specifics unless he inquired about them. I went on to ask the Greenmeadows salesman if any people who had moved in or signed up had asked about the issue. He thought for a few seconds and said he could not remember anyone who had, but he and several others said they were sure some people would say they never thought to ask, that they had just assumed we did not do this. I agreed that this would surely happen, but we had to be very consistent, even if it seemed artificial. I said our constant response to someone saying, "Why didn't you tell me you sold to Blacks?" has to be, "We answer every question truthfully. We assumed that if it mattered, you would ask about it."

Of course, when the Black couple followed the example of every home buyer and went out after work or on the weekend to see how their house was coming along, people who had already occupied or were similarly under contract would object. In Greenmeadows a few did, one of whom was a friend of mine since childhood, Bob Rosburg, a professional golfer. I had played hundreds of rounds of golf with him and had even defeated him in a local junior tournament. I knew his wife, who came from the South, and that he had three children. He had just moved in next door to the house the Black couple had selected and was concerned that his wife would be upset. I told him the decision was not reversible, explained that it was the right thing for us to do, and asked if he wanted me to talk with his wife. He said that wasn't necessary. I gave much the same explanation to six or seven others. Some grumbled and one or two were hostile, but once the couple moved in, the issue disappeared.

Early in the following year, we began construction of models and thirty additional houses in our first project in Marin County, Terra Linda, north of San Rafael, a large development, which had been initiated by another builder. He had put in site improvements for several hundred lots and built his models at the front end of the project. We bought sixty finished lots at the opposite end and optioned a few hundred others. By late spring we had finished and opened the models and completed several additional houses, twenty of which were occupied. Sales were going well. One day Bud Sthymmel, our salesman there, called to tell me he had a problem. A Black Air Force officer, a doctor stationed at Hamilton Field, which was about fifteen miles north of Terra Linda, had visited the project with his wife and signed up for a house scheduled for completion in about one month. Several people who had already moved in saw the couple and asked if we were going to sell to them. He said he already had, and they exploded and said they were going to call others who had moved in, as well as those who were in contract, to organize a joint protest. I told Bud to tell them I would come there the following Saturday at 11:00 AM, but before that to get me appointments with every resident who was not a member of the group.

On Saturday I talked with twelve couples in their homes. All were supportive, indifferent, or at most mildly upset. When I met with the group, it consisted of another twelve buyers, the leader of which was an Army colonel from the Presidio. They had a complaint and a fear. The complaint was that they had not been informed; their fear was of a decline in house values. Before directly addressing these two issues, I turned directly to the colonel and said, "I can understand that some people are apprehensive and want reassurance, but that you, an officer in the United States Army, should be their leader is disgraceful and quite possibly a violation of the Army code of conduct. I would like the name and telephone number of your commanding officer." I then gave the same explanation I had given to the Greenmeadows buyers six months earlier. It satisfied some and not others. During the week, Bud said that there was a request for another meeting. This time they wanted my father to come. When I told him of this, I recommended against his going, but he did not take my advice. There were about twenty people at the second meeting who expressed the same complaint and fear. The content of my father's response was similar to mine with one important exception. I had not addressed the request that we buy their houses back because it might give credence to their claim, but he did. Exuding power and confidence as I could not, he made it personal. "I would be glad to buy anybody's house back. We sold them too cheap anyway just because it was our initial effort here. You put less than $500 down, and I have millions invested here. Do you think I would sell to a Black couple if I thought it would drive down the value of my property?"

It was not so much the content of his declaration but its sheer force that broke the back of the opposition. Not everyone was fully satisfied. A few remained concerned, but no one took him up on his offer to buy the house back. In Greenmeadows there had been only a few weeks between contract and occupancy of the Black couple. In Terra Linda, the Black officer was two months away from discharge and could not close and occupy until then. Some grumbling continued, but it died down as soon as they moved in. These first two experiences convinced me that whenever possible, we should narrow the time between contract and occupancy when the buyer was Black. There was, however, one more case in which that was not possible. I shall relate the circumstances because they demonstrate how easily there can be a misunderstanding on the issue between a husband and a wife.

In 1959, we sold one of the model homes in the San Mateo Highlands, a large project in which we had been building for three years and in which we still owned several hundred lots. We had made some design changes to the existing models and had new ones under construction and scheduled for opening in about six weeks. We had sold the existing models for delivery when the new ones were ready. The buyers of one of them were a Black lawyer and his wife. The house on either side had also been sold. One day the salesman, Jonas Harschel, a man especially supportive of racial integration, called to warn me of an impending problem. The White husband, an airline pilot, who with his wife had contracted for an adjoining house, had seen the Black couple visiting and verbally attacked the salesman. "I didn't know you sold houses to Blacks, and I certainly didn't know one had bought next door to my house. I want my deposit back," he had shouted. Jonas had asked him why he had not asked about the subject. He had replied that it had never occurred to him. Jonas then offered him a house in a different part of the project, but he refused and again demanded the return of his $3,000 deposit. Jonas correctly declined to do that. Then the man asked him who his immediate boss was and got my name. A few hours later the pilot called me and we had a similar conversation.

After he hung up in anger, I went to the woman managing loan processing and closing, apprised her of the situation, and asked if the loan was ready for closing. She said it was, and I told her to be prepared for trouble with the customer. I forgot about the matter until two months later when I asked the loan manager what had happened with the pilot. "Oh," she said, "I guess I forgot to tell you. Three weeks ago I called to tell them that their house had been released for occupancy and set a date with them for closing, which they kept. I couldn't understand what all the fuss was about. They were very nice people and thrilled about finally being able to move into their house."

A few weeks later, I was driving by the house they had bought and saw a man in his fifties working in the front garden. I stopped, introduced myself, and told him I was curious about what had happened. I said, "After your angry statements to me and Jonas, and your threat to sue, you just calmly walked into our office and closed. Would you mind telling me what changed your mind and how you feel about the matter now?"

"Oh, sure," he said somewhat sheepishly. "I was recently married for the second time to a woman who is much younger than me and who grew up in the South. I didn't object to having a Black neighbor, certainly not when the husband is a lawyer, but I was terrified that my wife would be very upset. When you and Jonas wouldn't give me our deposit back, I had to tell her. When I did, she didn't seem interested. What she did want to talk about was what kind of drapes we were going to get and whether we should replace any of our furniture, which was traditional, with more contemporary stuff." Then he told me that he, his wife, and the Black neighbors had become good friends and invited me to come in and meet her. When I did, she went on and on telling me how much she liked the house.

I never kept track of the exact number of houses we sold to Blacks from 1954 to 1967, when the company went bankrupt. My guess is that it was about 3 percent of the roughly 7,000 houses we built in that period, or 200. Apart from the three cited above, I know of no serious incident about the matter, even though in 1959, my father decided to go public with our policy. The catalyst for this was a decision by the Supreme Court of California that banned discrimination in the sale or rental of housing. When this decision was announced, the executive director of the local home builders' association, of which we were one of the largest dues-paying members, was asked by a reporter for his opinion on it. He said, "It will be a disaster for the home-building industry in the state."

My father read this comment on his fifty-ninth birthday. After a party celebrating the event, my father, who was not entirely sober, took me into his study and asked me what I thought of what he called, in anger, "This jerk's ridiculous statement. What the hell is he doing replying at all without consulting me? After all, who else knows better than I do what the effect has been?"

I agreed that it was a silly and uncalled-for statement, but I told him I thought that we should continue our policy of not discussing our policy publicly. But I added, "It's your call."

He was silent for a few moments, and then he laughed and said, "What the hell. It's my birthday and I feel like having some fun. Let's draft a reply to this bastard, tell what our experience has been, and send it to the papers." We did that, and, of course, it got a lot of coverage, including even by *Time* magazine.

My father's reaction was entirely personal, as was the case with everything about Eichler Homes. The company, the houses, and his persona were inextricably intermingled. There was no separation among them. This was also true of Bill Levitt. They could hire people to manage certain activities like construction, purchasing, contracting, sales and marketing, and loan processing, but they would have no qualm about bypassing them to inquire of and give directions to lower-level employees. When challenged for doing so, especially by a son, their response would be the same. "It's my company, Goddamn it." And so it was.

I have often heard people say that Eichler Homes proved that selling homes to anyone without regard for race or ethnicity could be successful, that it even added sales. I have never made such a claim and do not make it now. We would have had less trouble and sold more houses if we had excluded Blacks. As was inevitable, real estate brokers handling resales and salespeople for competing builders regularly told prospects who indicated that they were considering buying an Eichler home, "Don't do that. They sell to Blacks [or worse]; that will hurt your resale value." On balance, we probably lost more sales than we gained. On the other hand, the negative effect was far less for us than it would have been for others, especially for Levitt. It made no contribution to the demise of Eichler Homes and appropriately enhanced the reputation of their creator.

Like other merchant builders in the 1950s and early 1960s, Larry Weinberg did not sell to Blacks, but, as I showed in the last chapter, unlike them, not doing so troubled him deeply. Donald Trump was different from all of them. The first time I met him, at the federally subsidized apartment project he and his father were building in Brooklyn, he bragged about avoiding the requirement that he rent to Blacks. "I hired Roy Cohn" he said, "and told him to find a way to get me out of selling to 'them.' And the son of a bitch did it. You should have seen Cohn browbeat the federal judge."

7

The Resurrectionist: Victor Palmieri

I first met Victor Palmieri in the late 1950s, when he was serving with my father on a California governor's commission charged with studying regional planning issues and making recommendations for action by the state and local governments. Two years later Pat Brown asked me to chair another commission, this time to make recommendations to him, the legislature, and the federal government on new policies to solve housing problems, the most important of which was better access to those discriminated against by their low incomes and/or their race. At the governor's request, his executive assistant, Charles O' Brien, met with me to go over a list of prospective members. It was immediately apparent that there were more interest groups that needed or hoped to have representation than the number of allocated slots could fill. As the head of a major development project in southern California, Janss/Conejo, and as a friend and supporter of the governor, Victor was on the list, and I strongly endorsed his appointment. This was the first of a series of involvements I had with Victor over the next three decades.

A few months later, when the commission was scheduled to hold hearings in Los Angeles, Victor invited me to spend the night at his house in Malibu. I accepted and met his wife, Tita, for the first time. After we had had dinner and Tita and their children had gone to bed, he and I stayed up for several hours talking, mostly about his ambitions, which were considerable. He wanted to be elected to a high office—for example, governor—to have the power to make real changes for the greater good of society. At first glance, he was well suited for the role. He had been editor of the _Law Review_ at Stanford University and knew many people of importance in the Democratic Party (he had switched parties in 1958 when Brown was elected governor); he was a close friend of rising young stars like Warren Christopher, the governor's first executive secretary and President Carter's secretary of state, and Bill Norris, who later became a judge. All of them unreservedly supported him. He was tall, well built, and handsome, and he carried himself well. And, of course, he was very smart. I had similar ambitions and had had more extensive contact with elected officials than he, but I was coming to the conclusion that I was unsuited for such a pursuit. Although not entirely for the same reasons, I thought he was too. Neither of us suffered fools well, but, unlike me, he appeared stiff.

When Victor graduated from law school, he and Warren Christopher joined the prestigious law firm O'Melveny & Meyer. One of his clients there was Ed Janss, who along with his brother, Bill, was heir to a fortune. Their father, a doctor, had acquired two large parcels of land in the area, one of which became Westwood and the site of UCLA. Early in the 1900s, the board of regents had decided to seek a location for a second campus and sent a committee to southern California to review alternative sites. There was a story, never confirmed, that Dr. Janss bribed their driver to tout his property. In any event, if you walk the streets of Westwood today, you will see the name "Janss" embedded in the sidewalks. The other parcel, the Conejo Ranch, was 10,000 acres thirty-five miles northwest on the road to Santa Barbara. The Janss family bred horses on it, and it was often used as a location for Western movies. By 1950, Westwood, UCLA, and much of the surrounding land had been fully developed, including Century City. Most of it was once owned by Janss. Now the urban boundary was moving west toward the Conejo Ranch. Once again, a Janss holding was ripe for development.

I am not sure whether Victor persuaded Ed Janss to initiate development of the ranch or whether it had already happened before he became the family's lawyer. I do know that by 1961, he had left the law firm and taken charge of this process, which was by then moving forward rapidly. A master plan for the whole property, including a golf course, housing, offices, and a regional shopping center, had been approved by Ventura County. The golf course was built and operating, an extensive road network had been installed, and several merchant builders were constructing and selling houses there.

While all this was proceeding under Victor's direction, he was making plans for an expansion of Janss's corporation into other development ventures outside California. By 1962, the company had built a six-story office building at the Santa Monica Airport for its burgeoning staff, had bought Sun Valley (Bill Janss was an ardent skier), and was buying and/or taking options on sites for recreational use in several other areas distant from southern California. Aware at the time that I was in serious conflict with my father, Victor made me a tempting offer. He asked if I would take a one-year leave from Eichler Homes to supervise the planning of a large parcel at the Conejo Ranch for high-density, low-rise, sales housing and get the plan approved by the county. He proposed to pay me $40,000 for half of my time, about the same annual salary I was receiving at Eichler Homes. I could devote the other half of my time to the ongoing work of the State Housing Commission, which was mandated to deliver a report by the middle of 1963. I accepted and moved with my wife and two young boys to West Los Angeles. I had been giving my father such a bad time that he was relieved to have me take a sabbatical. As if I had planned it, which I had not, the first day I walked into the Santa Monica office and introduced myself to the receptionist, clearly awed, she said, "Oh, Mr. Eichler, the governor has been trying to reach you."

I finished the job Victor had asked me to do in five months. When I told him this, he said, "Why not just hang around and be available to talk with me when I feel like it? I need someone smart and from outside my organization who will give me unbiased advice." I agreed, but a few weeks later my father and mother came to have dinner at our home. After the children were in bed, he handed me a written proposal under which I was to return to Eichler Homes and have complete control of the single-family part of the business. He would confine himself solely to the high-rise apartments. I was both attracted and wary, and I said I would think about the idea.

The next day I told Victor what my father had proposed and said that I thought I should do it. He said, "Get in the car with me. We're going for a drive." In near total silence, we went out to the Conejo Project and parked under a tree at the edge of the golf course. Then he turned to me and said, "You know damn well your father won't keep the agreement. He may mean it now, but he can't live with it. Eichler Homes is too much his. So tell me what you really want to do."

I thought about this for a few minutes and said, "I would like to build houses on my own, but I don't have any money to get started."

He pointed to the parcel of land I had just gotten planned and approved and said, "Why don't you do it there? We'll do a joint venture. We'll contribute the land, pay for the site improvements, and sign the construction loans; you get the houses designed, built, and sold, and we'll split the profits." I took a few days to consider both proposals and decided to go back to Eichler Homes. In less than six months, my father broke the deal, and I left the company to run a study project at UC–Berkeley. Victor had been right.

The next time I talked to Victor was almost a decade later, when he asked me to work on his new contract with Penn Central. I have already described some incidents in that activity involving Victor (see Chapter I), but there is one which I did not mention then and which bears on an inherent conflict in Victor's character. One afternoon in 1976, at Victor's request, I met with him at the town house he was then occupying in Manhattan. As soon as I got there, he told me an amazing story. His contract with the Penn Central trustees to manage the Pennsylvania Company provided for an incentive fee of 5 percent of the increase from its appraised value then to its value five years later. If the company was not sold at that time, the value was to be determined by another appraisal, presumably performed by the trustees' investment banking adviser, Lehman Brothers. The end of the five-year term was at least a year away, but for reasons having nothing to do with the VPCO contract, Lehman had been instructed to appraise many of the Penn Central assets, including the Pennsylvania Company. Based on that appraisal the VPCO incentive fee was $20 million, at least half of which would go to Victor.

Instead of being elated at this circumstance, Victor seemed troubled. I asked him why this was so. He then explained what I already knew, that one of the major assets the trustees would sell to reimburse creditors would be a stripped-down, profitable railroad freight operation. What I did not know was that Victor hoped that the trustees would appoint him to be the CEO of that company before they put it up for sale. He not only told me that but also went on to say that one of the trustees, John MacArthur, dean of the Harvard Business School and his friend, had told him that it would terribly embarrass the trustees if VPCO was paid what everyone would view as a windfall. He told Victor that the terms of the contract had to be altered and the amount of the fee reduced. I interrupted Victor at this point and asked, "If the contract was properly drawn and approved, and it was, and even if, as is likely, the trustees are criticized, there can be only one reason for you to accede to this demand. That is your own feeling that you and your partners did a lousy job. If, as I assume, you performed very well, better than anyone else could have done, if your skill resulted in the maximum value increase that the admittedly improved economic conditions facilitated, you should tell MacArthur you are getting exactly what you deserve. After all, his constituents, the creditors, are getting 95 percent of the value increase."

Victor pondered these remarks and then said, "That is all true, but I will lose something if I act on it. Some time ago I told MacArthur that I would like to be the CEO of the restructured railroad company. Now he says that if I don't agree to a lower fee, I won't have a chance to get that job."

I was surprised that Victor would even take such a position, let alone seek it. I said, "It doesn't suit you; it doesn't use your best talents. If you want to run a company, start one or buy a small one with the money you get from Penn Central. You would find it boring to manage a railroad company."

Whether or not my advice had any effect, Victor did not reduce the incentive and did not become CEO of the railroad company, but his next step suggests that the desire to do something different, something that was both important and visible, remained unsatisfied. With the Levitt trusteeship over and John Koskinen ably running the Penn Central real estate disposition program, Victor responded to an offer from his friend, Warren Christopher, then deputy secretary of state. Christopher proposed that he take on the job of ambassador at large for refugee affairs. Unfortunately for Victor, he accepted and was soon buried by the impossible task of dealing with the boat people, refugees fleeing Cuba. As he was struggling with this, VPCO was awarded a contract to restructure assets of the notorious Teamsters Union Pension Fund.

By the mid-1980s, the Penn Central and Teamster projects were finished or at least winding down, and Victor had remarried a much younger woman, Rhonda, who had founded a small, avant-garde ballet company in San Francisco where the couple now lived. My wife, Audrey, and I had Victor and his wife to dinner one night. After they left, Audrey said, "That woman is all wrong for Victor. He should be married to someone much more glamorous, a star like Diane Sawyer."

Incidentally, when Audrey had first met Victor at a party in New York several years earlier, it was the only time I had ever heard him refer to his parents or to being Italian. Audrey's father had been Italian. He looked at her carefully and said, "You remind me of my mother. She was from Bari [a city on the eastern coast of Italy]."

A few months after he had been at our house, Victor called me and asked if I would come to his apartment for dinner. He said his wife would be out; it would be just the two of us. When I arrived, he served me a drink and said he wanted to discuss two subjects. First, he told me he had received a grant from the Ford Foundation to write a book on his experiences with the Cuban refugees and said, "I have been trying to do it for a few months and just can't seem to get into it. I know you have written two books and wondered how you went about it."

I replied, "There are many men who are highly intelligent, who have had interesting experiences, and who are quite literate, but who just can't write about them. My father was that way. To my surprise, I discovered that I can make a list of chapters and a schedule for writing them and pretty well stick to it, but that doesn't make me a better man than you. You have accomplished many things I couldn't do. I suggest that you forget the whole thing and give the foundation its money back."

Victor just shrugged his shoulders as if to say, "That's what I thought, but I hoped I was wrong."

Looking back, I realize that this was a kind of segue into the next subject. Victor told me he had received a request from Max Karl, founder of MGIC, the first nongovernmental company to insure mortgages on single-family homes. It had become very successful, gone public, and merged with Baldwin United, which had diversified from its original business of making pianos into financial services. This diversification had brought the company close to insolvency. According to Victor, Karl had asked him to join the company. If he did, Karl said, he would be given a free hand. Victor wanted to know if I thought he should do it. I'd never met Karl, but I knew quite a bit about him and the mortgage insurance business. I told him that Karl was desperate, as are most founders, especially those whose companies are failing. "Hell," I said, "he's just like my father. When I told you he had offered to give me autonomy in the single-family part of Eichler Homes, you said, 'He won't do it; he can't do it.' And you were right." I went on to say that he was proposing to violate two conditions that had to obtain before taking over a sick company. First, it should have reached the bottom of its decline. Second, and even more important, there had to be a change in power, preferably one ordered by a court. After talking to the then CEO and the creditors, Victor apparently reached the same conclusion at the time but later entered into a management contract with the company.

In retrospect, I think the middle and late 1980s may have been the worst period in Victor's life. As he later acknowledged, he had entered into a bad second marriage and was out of place in San Francisco, where he had few friends and where hardly anyone knew him. When I went home after that meeting at his apartment, I told my wife, who was a fan of Victor, that some of his remarks and his demeanor were suggestive of a movie star who had gone out of fashion. After all, he had been a figure of note, especially in Los Angeles and New York for over twenty years. To him, the future must have seemed bleak. In reality, however, his best years were ahead of him. By 1990, he had remarried, this time to a compatible woman, and moved back to New York. Of equal importance, he had found a new niche for his talents. Mutual Benefit Life Insurance Company had been placed in receivership largely because of bad investments in real estate. Initially, VPCO was brought in solely to deal with the real estate, but soon Victor discovered that there were problems with the insurance side of the business as well. Soon he was appointed to restructure other insurance companies. In other words, not only had he added an entirely new line of business, dealing with insurance issues, but he was to become known as *the* specialist at it. He also became chairman of two prestigious organizations, the finance committee of the Rockefeller Fund and the Lincoln Center Theater Company.

In 1991, I had dinner with Victor and his wife, Cathryn, in the loft in Soho he had bought many years earlier. There was a Henry Moore sculpture in the living room. Cathryn was an executive with Korn/Ferry, tall, red-haired, attractive, and intelligent. She was clearly in love with Victor, as he was with her. They had a house in the Hamptons, where they were spending much time playing golf. After leaving, I walked by myself and felt both happy for Victor and a little envious. My twenty-three-year marriage to Audrey was falling apart, and while I had built a successful business of my own over the previous nine years, its future was uncertain. I felt much the same as Victor must have six years earlier. I, too, would find yet another and better business success and a far better wife, but then Victor was always a decade or so ahead of me.

8

Private Lives

In the winter of 1959, I was in the Bahamas with my wife attending a meeting of the Young Turks, an organization of about twenty home builders formed by Ed Birkner, an editor of _House and Home_ magazine, a Luce publication. Ordinarily the meetings were held every two or three months at the location of one of the members. This time, Birkner had decided to invite the top executives of firms that sold to builders to mingle with a few of their customers. It was at this meeting that Martin Meyer, CFO of Certenteed Products Company, told me of his interest in acquiring Eichler Homes. On the day before the sessions were to start, I went to the airport to greet two partners from San Diego, Harvey Furgatch and Marty Gleich, with whom I had become friendly. As they came off the plane, I asked Harvey, "How is business?"

He responded with his own question, "Before or after bullshit?"

When I turned to Marty, I noticed that he was carrying a book about the Danish philosopher Kierkegaard and recalled that his own house was of excellent modern design. I asked, "Marty, how can someone with such good taste in literature and architecture build such mundane houses?"

Without hesitation, he replied, "Ned, I never impose my personal taste on my business. I sell houses at a good price which appeal to my buyers."

A year or so later, the group broke up, and I had no further contact with Marty or Harvey until I called each of them to conduct interviews for this book. I learned that they had ended their partnership in 1970 and had separately built houses for sale for several more years until both stopped. Neither as partners nor on their own had they ever considered merging or going public. Marty is eighty-one, three years older than Harvey. They both grew up in Bronx, New York, and knew each other as children, but Marty's family was wealthier and higher-class than Harvey's. His father was a doctor. He got a degree in civil engineering at Cornell and then worked for a few years for general contractors and home builders in New Jersey. Harvey went to a city college for only a year and then worked in small retail stores.

In 1951, Marty went to Washington, D.C., to do research on a special government program for the construction of military housing. He wanted to know how it worked and the best place to do it. He decided it was Houston, and he, his wife, and his friend Harvey, who was not married, "stuffed ourselves and our belongings into an old station wagon and set off for Houston, a place where none of us had ever been. After three weeks, my wife and I decided this was no place for us, and we moved on to San Diego, which also seemed a good place for the business we had chosen to enter. Having no money, Harvey stayed to work in a retail store until I could get things going. In a few months I called to tell him I needed him. He said, 'I'll come only if you are not trying to do me a favor.' I assured him I was not, and he came. In less than a year we concluded that the military housing program was too screwed up and started building houses for sale. We did that together for the next twenty years."

In the early 1960s, Marty turned much of the day-to-day management of the business over to Harvey and devoted most of his time to two pursuits. One was racing his boat, and the other was pursuing an education in the humanities. He took courses in philosophy, poetry, and Shakespeare at the University of California, San Diego. Most merchant builders used their own names for their companies. Harvey and Marty did not. Instead, they adopted the name American Housing Guild. I asked Marty whether this was because the names Furgatch and Gleich were not euphonious or because they were too Jewish for a conservative place like San Diego, which at the time had few Jews. He said these factors might have played a part in the decision, but that his main motive was to use the word *guild* for marketing reasons. "It had a nice ring, reminding people of the guilds in the Middle Ages," he said. I suggested he might be the only merchant builder who knew enough about history to have thought of such an association. In 1970, Marty decided to undertake a major geographic expansion. He had already made his brother-in-law, Mike Podell, a partner and sent him to the Bay Area and hired a regional manager for Los Angeles. Now he selected managers to run several eastern locations. Harvey, who, after leaving Houston, had become a full partner in the hugely successful San Diego operation, had no stomach for the new policy. He and Marty broke up. Later in the decade he reentered merchant building on his own only in and around San Diego.

By 1975, Marty knew that the expansion effort had failed and abandoned both it and home building. He has never returned to it. He did, however, retain ownership of a single-family mortgage business, which was also called Guild. It was initially created only to handle loans for the purchase of the company's houses. But after 1975, it sought other customers. That business, Guild Mortgage, occupies much of Marty's time today for two reasons. First, his three children are grown and have their own families. While his relationships with all of them and his wife are sound, they cannot keep him busy. Second, over the last ten years he has gradually lost most of his ability to see. As a result, he cannot race his boat or do the reading for formal courses. I asked him why, at the age of eighty-one, he bothers overseeing the mortgage business. "You don't need the money. Why not try to write?" I asked.

He replied, "Ned, I'm not like you. I just can't write. When I had to write theses for the courses I was taking, my wife read them and was appalled. 'You think so clearly,' she said, 'but it does not show when you write.' Many years ago she said something significant about me. When I complained that I had too much to do, she said, 'For you, the only thing worse than having too much to do is having nothing to do.' So coming to the office and looking over the shoulder of my manager gives me something to do."

As long as Marty and Harvey knew each other and as successful as they were at building houses, they have very different personalities. They have drifted apart over the last thirty years. Harvey also had outside interests, but they were different from those of his former partner. In the 1980s, he got very involved in owning and racing horses and served on the local racing commission. He also became active in politics. He and his wife were divorced many years ago, and he never remarried or had a serious relationship with another woman. When I asked him why this was so, he said, "You know, Ned, I'm just not cut out for marriage or being tied down with a woman. I'm too independent. I love to travel, and when I get the urge to go somewhere, I just pick up and go. I don't want to have to check in with a woman. I have even given up the racing and politics to be free of responsibilities." I asked if he had children and, if he did, how his relationship is with them. He replied, "I've got three. They are all married and have children, and I am very close to them and their families. In fact, one of my major activities is taking them all on trips." Lastly I asked what he did with himself to keep busy. "Do? I live," he exclaimed. "Besides, planning those trips is a lot of work. And I love doing it."

Harvey and Marty are different from each other in significant respects, but both of them are also different from any other men portrayed in this book. They did not put their own names on their product and never considered going public or merging. Conducting business or making money was not the central purpose of their lives. Harvey opposed geographic expansion, and Marty abandoned it quickly when he realized it was unworkable. Had he not lost his sight, he probably would not have needed to be active in the mortgage business in order to have something to do. He could have raced his boat and read. Harvey had one goal for his business: to make enough money to support himself and his other interests. Not born into a family with money, he assumed at the outset that that would be difficult to attain. When I interviewed him, he expressed his surprise at having been wrong: "Who knew it would be so easy to make a lot of money building houses in San Diego?"

Today, at least, neither Harvey nor Marty takes himself seriously. A week after an initial interview with each of them, I made second calls to each to check on some facts. I reached Marty, and he gave me the information I needed. I asked whether he would like me to send him a draft so that he could verify its accuracy. After a short pause, he said, "No, I don't want to read drafts. Send me an autographed copy of the book if you get it published."

When I called Harvey, I got his answering machine, "This is the bearded man with the cap. Leave a message." I did leave a message, but he never called back. I am neither surprised nor upset. He had already answered my questions. Why should he spend any more time on the matter? If I got something wrong, it would make no difference to him. Nothing I write could affect his enjoyment of the life he worked so hard to attain. Everyone else about whom I have written took himself seriously. Marty and Harvey are refreshing exceptions.

9

Contrasts in Success: Eli Broad and Harold Blumenstein

I emphasize here a point that I hope has already been clear to the reader. I give a far broader meaning to the word _fortune_ than just acquiring a lot of money. As used here, it implies achieving a life balanced among other activities, especially, but not limited to, family and recreation. Measured by that standard, Weinberg, Furgatch, Gleich, and Palmieri were more successful than Trump, Levitt, or my father. As I progressed, however, the work has had two unintended dimensions. First, I have chosen to deal only with people I knew. Second, with the exception of Palmieri and Trump, the subjects are all Jewish. There certainly are and have been many Gentile merchant builders, but I do not know enough about them firsthand to present their stories. In this chapter I shall introduce a third element on which I had not intended to focus, business ethics, by comparing the practices of two men, Harold Blumenstein and Eli Broad, both of whom, ironically, grew up in the Detroit area, but never knew each other. In addition to living by different ethical standards, they contrast sharply in their respective attitudes toward fame. One is an intensely private man; the other has become a public figure.

Eli Broad

I first met Eli Broad in the late 1950s, when Eichler Homes was at or near its peak. I do not recall the venue or the occasion, but what he said always stuck in my mind. I did know that he had been building homes in the Detroit area, that he had shifted his operation to southern California, that he catered to the low end of the market, that he built relatively small projects, and that if there had been a partner named Kaufman, he remained in Detroit. At out meeting Eli asked me who financed our construction, and I said mainly savings and loans. With obvious contempt, he shot back, "I would never do that. It is too expensive. I use commercial banks. They're much cheaper."

I replied that I knew that, but that we, like most builders, were always short of money and could get larger loans from savings and loans and treated the extra cost as payment for working capital. I asked, "Where do you get yours?"

I had expected him to say he had brought his own money into the business or had gotten it from his family or private investors, but he did not. Instead, he answered, "I get it from subcontractors and suppliers."

I assumed he meant that he had created a kind of "cooperative" and asked, "How exactly do you do that?"

He replied, "I just take a long time paying them. My working capital is the money I owe them."

I said that we and other builders selectively delayed paying subs and suppliers who could afford to wait when we were short of money, but that I knew of no one who did it as a policy. Then I asked, "Don't a lot of them go broke?"

He said, "Sure, but I can always replace them."

My next insight was into how Eli treated employees. It came secondhand in 1975. By then, his company had gone public, expanded into several areas, suffered a decline in earnings, and made a longtime employee, Eugene Rosenfeld, president. He remained chairman. At the time, I was president of Levitt. One day Jim Klingbeil, for whom I had worked from 1968 to 1972, called me to say that he and Rosenfeld had formed a partnership to build single-family homes and would like to acquire some Levitt lots in Chicago. I told him that might be possible, and we agreed to meet a week later. When we did, I told Gene, whom I knew, that I had not heard that he had left Kaufman and Broad and asked why he did so after being with the company so long and having risen so far through the ranks. He said, "I have a pretty thick skin and am fairly tolerant of abuse, but working for Eli became impossible. I can't tell you how glad I am to be out of there."

My last two encounters with Eli were direct and also occurred while I was at Levitt. The first had to do with our operation in France. As mentioned in Chapter III, Kaufman and Broad and Levitt were then the only two American firms building homes in France. In fact, when I was in Paris, I had a drink with Bruce Karatz, K and B's regional manager there. When he asked me how things were going, I told him that I had fired our manager in France and was looking for a replacement. He said, "How about me? I'll consider it for the right price."

Since he was aware that I knew Eli, this seemed odd, but soon I discovered that he only wanted to learn more about our holdings. Before the sale of Levitt

France to the employees, we had put it on the open market. One day John Kosk-inen called me and said, "I have been talking to Eli Broad about his buying Levitt France. We have agreed on a price and he wants to me to bring a lawyer and meet him at the Hyatt O'Hare next week to sign a deal. I'd like you to come along." I told John that Eli was a slippery character and asked if he thought all the terms were settled. He said they were.

I then asked, "Why the hell are all of us flying off to Chicago to sign a deal for a company in France? Why doesn't he come to New York or Washington, or why don't we just do the deal by mail or fax?" John said that Eli was very busy, could meet in Chicago on only one day next week, and wanted to get the deal done quickly. I was skeptical but agreed to attend the meeting.

When John, our lawyer, and I walked into the meeting at the appointed hour of 2:00 PM, Bruce Karatz was the only person there, not Eli and not a K and B lawyer. Karatz said, "Eli was held up and will be here in about two hours. I am sorry about that, but it will give me some time to go over some questions I have. I told Eli I think the price might be too high."

Before John could express his own dismay, I said to him, "Come on, let's get out of here. I told you we can't do business with these guys."

Having more patience than I, John said, "What the hell, we have come this far, let's see if we can make a deal." For two and a half hours, Karatz asked ques-tions that had already been answered and expressed skepticism about the price.

When Eli finally arrived, he issued a perfunctory apology and asked Karatz, "How do you feel about the deal now?" Karatz repeated his mantra. By then even John had had enough. We said good-bye and left. I never again heard from Eli about France, but, as mentioned in Chapter III, he did call me at home when Levitt itself was offered for sale to ask how he might get a good deal.

Over the next three decades Eli Broad became very rich and well-known, not just among people who followed merchant building. His company acquired an insurance company, Sun Life of Canada, which later was spun off and specialized in investments for retirees. It and the home-building company, whose name was changed to KB Homes, grew and made excellent profits. Eli has been listed in the Forbes 400, is a major collector of modern art, and is a contributor to and board member of major art museums. He also gives large sums of money to universities and other worthy institutions. He is a living testament to the proposition that conducting unethical business is no bar to success and may even be conducive to achieving it, nor does it prevent one from being admired for activities in other fields, especially when it involves making large donations.

Harold Blumenstein

It would be difficult to imagine a successful businessman whose character is more different from Eli Broad's than Harold Blumenstein. The best evidence of that is that very few people have ever heard of him. He is about ten years younger than Eli, has lived his entire life in and around Detroit, has made a great deal of money, mostly in residential development, is intensely private, regularly spends and enjoys time with his wife of more than thirty years and his three grown children and their families, is passionately devoted to his several business activities, collects modern art, races vintage cars, travels extensively, skis, plays golf, has a wonderful sense of humor, which includes laughing at himself, and is the most principled businessman I have ever known.

I met Harold by accident in 1992. He invested in and became a partner of a business I had founded ten years earlier. This new phase of my business succeeded far more than either of us had expected. Four years later, when I had reached the age of sixty-six and had just concluded a painful divorce, at my request, he bought my share and I retired. A brief depiction of how this happened and what it says about the unique character of this man will, I hope, enlighten and even entertain the reader without violating Harold's penchant for privacy.

In spring 1992, I was a few months into an attempt to raise the $6.5 million I needed to complete the new capital requirement of Fannie Mae to participate in its DUS (Designated Underwriting and Servicing) apartment mortgage program. Under its provisions, a qualified mortgage banker can originate loans without prior approval and earn a higher-than-normal servicing fee if he has the necessary capital and is willing to share in the credit risk. I had been operating successfully in the program in a joint venture with an already approved firm for two years, but Fannie Mae asked me to apply for my own license. The capital requirement had been raised from $2.5 million to $7.5 million. I had only $1 million in qualified capital and had never been good at raising money for my own ventures. Through a friend, I found a young lawyer from Florida, Steve Fayne, who was interested both in making an investment and joining the operation. He thought he could raise the money in Florida. To do so, he prepared an offering circular for a "Private Placement" (an SEC term) solicitation, which is restricted to investors who live in a single state and have significant net worth. We gained commitments for only $3.5 million in the next three months. Concurrently, I had made contact with three entities in the Northeast who were interested in making the entire investment and was about to leave on a trip to visit each one of them. A day before my departure, as I was having lunch with my wife on the deck of our San

Francisco home, the phone rang. I answered and a male voice said, "This is Harold Blumenstein. I am calling from Michigan and want to ask you some questions about your offering circular."

I was surprised and asked him how he had gotten the offering circular in Michigan and why he was calling me in San Francisco (Fayne had been listed as the contact person). He said that his partner, Dennis Rogers, had been playing golf in Florida, met a stranger, a local lawyer, on the course, and asked him if he knew of any local real estate investment opportunities. Fayne had been temporarily sharing an office with this man and had given him the offering circular. The man tossed it onto the backseat of his car and forgot about it. The lawyer gave the circular to Rogers, who gave it to Harold, who was now calling me. Having long believed that there was such a thing as fate, I concluded that it must have had a hand in such an improbable set of circumstances. I told Harold to ask his questions. The DUS program was arcane and I had had a difficult time explaining its provisions to prospective investors. Most of them also were having a hard time believing that I could have done so much business without having any losses or delinquencies. In twenty minutes Harold asked better and more pointed questions than any of the other interested investors had asked in hours. When he finished, he asked if my record would stand up to careful scrutiny. I said it would. Then he said that he was very interested, but only if he and his partner could have the entire $6.5 million. He went on to ask when I could come to his office in Birmingham, Michigan, a suburb of Detroit, to meet with him and Dennis Rogers for a further discussion. As improbable as this seemed, it rang true to me. I said I was going east to see prospective investors and could fit in a meeting with him only on the following Friday. He said he would check with Rogers on availability and call me back in a few minutes. When he did, he said that Friday was fine. I told him I would bring Steve Fayne.

We met in Rogers' office at a small, round conference table. He and Harold each had copies of the offering circular and used it as a guide for the questions they asked. As they turned each page, he or Dennis put questions to me. They showed no interest in the proposed structure of the deal or the profit split, which was 50/50, but concentrated entirely on the nature of the business itself and the use of their investment, which was to be held in a separate account, bear interest, and be drawn on only to cover losses greater than the company's available funds. We had started at 9:00 AM. An hour and a half later they turned over the last page and said they were finished with their questions. I said I wanted to know something about them. Their story follows.

They had formed a partnership thirty years earlier to build garden apartments and later also suburban office/industrial complexes. They had never had a written agreement and none of their children had ever been in their business. They had sold the office buildings recently to an insurance company at a substantial profit but retained 5,000-plus apartments, which they managed themselves. Dennis had recently retired and was spending most of his time in Florida. He told me that I would never see him again unless things go wrong. They had stopped building apartments a few years earlier because the numbers didn't work and were seeking an investment in a related activity. Despite the periodic market difficulties that had prevailed over thirty years, they had never had a late payment or a default on a mortgage, including the one loan they had done with Fannie Mae. Their financial statements were almost identical, showing substantial net worth, cash in the bank, and marketable securities. They had no debt except mortgages secured by the apartments. When I later called the two largest banks in Detroit, with whom they did business, each officer said, "If our board said we could lend only to two existing clients, I would have picked Dennis and Harold."

By 11:00 AM, we had run out of questions about each other or the mortgage operation, so I turned to the deal itself. I told Harold that I assumed that he would want some control over loan quality and that both of us would want a divorce provision if either became dissatisfied with the arrangement. He agreed. I then asked what other information he would need to decide if he wanted to proceed. He asked, "Will all the statements in the circular and that you have made today check out?" I said that they would. He then said, "Subject to that and working out the details of the two provisions you just mentioned, we are ready to commit the money. It's up to you."

I thought about what kind man I had just met and decided that I should trust him to be straight and fair. "On the first," I said, "let's keep it simple. We'll have a three-man loan committee, myself, you, and Sherman Maisel, a finance professor and former governor of the Federal Reserve Board, who had served on our former loan committee. You will have a veto on any loan. If I think you are using it capriciously, I can end the partnership. In other words, each of us will have the right to terminate." He agreed and I said, "I was supposed to fly from here to the East for three other appointments. If you want to proceed, get your lawyer and we'll lock him and Steve in a hotel room and tell them to produce a full agreement by tomorrow morning. If we do that, I'll cancel my other meetings and fly home tomorrow afternoon." And that is what we did.

In the next four years we originated $1.4 billion in mortgages, none of which had a delinquency, let alone a default. Harold occasionally rejected a loan, but it usually happened before a meeting of the loan committee, which met by telephone. When I thought a prospective loan might bother Harold, I called him to get his opinion on it. Sometimes he convinced me that we should drop it; other times he agreed that the loan was okay. Either way, we saved processing time and effort. Twice Maisel objected to a loan, and we did not do it. Dry as this process sounds, I looked forward to the meetings to hear Harold's humorous analogies. Most of them were responses to an underwriter or a salesman talking about a prospect. Here are just three of many examples:

Salesman: I am working on a guy who has a great loan but wants a discount on the fee. I'm not sure he'll apply even if we give it to him.

Harold: Are you sure he won't do the loan even if we give him the discount?

Salesman: Why do you want to know that?

Harold: I'm like the butcher when a woman asks him if he has lamb chops. When he says yes, she asks how much for a pound. He says $10. She says the butcher across the street sells them for $5 a pound. He asks her why she doesn't buy them there. She says because he's out of them. The butcher says, "Lady, when I'm out of lamb chops, I sell them for $5 a pound, too."

Sales Manager: I'm working with the salesman on a loan for a very prominent family from Cleveland. I've underwritten the loan at a maximum of $4 million and they want another $100,000.

Harold: I know those people. They spill that much change from their pockets in a week. Stick to the $4 million. They'll do the loan.

Harold: I think the loan amount is high.

Underwriter: But it's only 75 percent of the appraisal.

Harold: The appraiser will be the high bidder at the foreclosure sale.

These remarks, delivered without a moment's hesitation, are signs not just of wit but of a very fast mind. But what is much more admirable about Harold are two principles he sets for himself in conducting business: being paid only what he has bargained for and keeping his word. The following are examples of each. We had arranged a joint venture with a privately owned bank, under which we would originate $400 million in "small" ($500,000 to $1,500,000) loans, and the bank would accumulate them, securitize them with Fannie Mae, and sell them. We would retain the servicing as part of our share of the proceeds. The matter went as planned, but the day after the loans were sold to outside investors, a junior executive of the bank called me and said, "There was a clerical error in the documentation of the sale, which you had no part in, but Lehman Brothers, who bought most of the package for a client, is in big trouble. The papers have to be redrawn and you have to sign them as the servicing agent. There is no risk to you, but I think you can hold Lehman up for some money."

It would not have occurred to me to do that, but I asked him how much, and he said at least $50,000. I said I would discuss the matter with Harold and get back to him. I called Harold and told him the story. He asked if I was sure there was no risk to us. I said I was. Then he said, "I don't want one Goddamn cent I am not entitled to. Sign the papers."

Ironically, several months later the same young man at the same bank told me that his boss had instructed him to renegotiate the profit split. He said that our share was too rich. I said we had made an agreement and expected his boss to live up to it. When they insisted on reducing our share, Harold sued them. The bank executive immediately called me and suggested that he and I should be able to settle the suit before everyone spent a lot of money on lawyers. I told him that the only reason I would do this was that Harold had driven a vintage car off a cliff in Mexico, had badly injured his back, had refused to let the doctor put a rod in his back or take pain pills, and insisted that he would fully recover by engaging in very painful physical therapy. "I am not as principled as Harold," I said. "I'll toss you a bone to get you off the hook with your boss, to save legal costs and not bother Harold." After two weeks of negotiation, I gave him my last offer, $25,000 off the amount we were owed, which I was not sure Harold would accept. He said he could not take this to his boss. I then said, "Okay, I tried. You are now going to find out what it is like to deal with Harold when he knows he's right. It won't be about the money with him, it will be about a principle, that your boss should keep his word."

Several months later the young man called me and was crying. "You were right," he said, "I got my boss down to $10,000, and Harold would not budge. I just got fired."

The mortgage company had a line of credit to "warehouse" (fund and hold) loans for a few days between the closing and Fannie Mae funding. It was very safe, but most banks did not understand that. Harold had convinced Detroit National Bank to take it on, and it was working smoothly for us and profitably for them. As the line was reaching its annual expiration date, Bear Stearns asked our CFO, my son Steven, if they could bid the line. Steven had had considerable dealings with them for us on another matter. It was not clear to me or Harold why Bear Stearns wanted the business, but Steven persuaded us to let them make a bid. When they did, their price was about the same as Detroit National's. Harold and I agreed we should keep the line where it was. A week later, Steven called me to say that Bear Stearns just offered to do the line at a much lower cost to us. The annual saving was about $500,000. I said, "There is one question which has to be answered before we even consider this. Did Harold commit us to the bank?" He said he did not know, and I asked him to set up a three-way telephone call. When he did and told Harold of the situation, I asked him, "I know the papers haven't been drawn, but did you give your word to the bank?"

He said, "Well, I told them to draw the papers, which has not been done."

I then said, "Harold, only you can answer this question. Did you feel that by saying that you were making a commitment?" There was a long pause, during which I could feel Harold's dilemma. He didn't want to make his partner suffer for his desire to keep his word. I told Steven to thank Bear Stearns but to say we were already committed.

I do not know where Harold got his unusual insistence on conducting business according to these principles, but I look upon the four years in which I was his partner as the best working experience I ever had. I never tire of telling others about his exemplary character and his wonderful stories and remarks. His early choice to build apartments for rent rather than homes for sale may well have stemmed from his desire to be private. By its nature, merchant building requires the owner to become a public figure.

10

Aftermath: Merchant Building

In 1982, the MIT Press published my second book, *Merchant Building*. I concluded it by predicting that the fortunes of home building in general and firms operating in many geographic areas in particular would be squeezed by economic and political circumstances. There were good reasons at the time for believing that. Interest rates had risen sharply from 1978 onward, causing margins and volume to shrink. The Fed's decision in 1981 to break the back of inflation and institute a recession only made matters worse. By throwing money at builders, banks and savings and loans created a housing surplus and many of them failed. However, these conditions and the way the Fed reacted to them laid the groundwork for a steady increase in the production of sales housing and, of equal or greater importance, an acceleration of price rises. Concurrently, the dramatic losses had made depository institutions reluctant to make loans for the purchase and development of land and for house construction. For the first time in history, the benefits of access to patient capital by going public outweighed the inherent inefficiencies of being large, multicity producers. The excess overhead caused by having two oversight organizations, one at the headquarters and another in each region, still more than offset any savings from large-scale purchasing. But at least now, it would be unlikely that a regional manager would able to go to a bank or an S and L and say, "I'm the guy who gets everything done. All I get from headquarters is silly orders and an overhead charge on top of mine. Lend me the money to buy land and build houses, and we'll both win."

Near the end of the 1980s, when many commercial banks were in serious trouble, Alan Greenspan's Fed adopted a risky, but nevertheless successful, strategy to save them from themselves. It kept short-term interest rates low and permitted and even encouraged depository institutions to eschew questionable lending in favor of buying long-term high-grade bonds. He was telling them, "I'd rather have you gambling on the yield curve—that is, borrowing short and lending long—than making risky loans." An unintended consequence of this was a reduction in rates on home mortgages. Concurrently, investment banks were perfecting the process of securitizing mortgages—that is, accumulating large numbers of loans and selling bonds secured by them. There were two ways by which these bonds could get a high credit rating. One was having a so-called agency (Freddie Mac or Fannie Mae) guarantee each loan. The other was having the entire package rated by Standard and Poors or Moodys. The latter required large pools of mortgages diversified geographically. Only a national home builder would have the financial ability to accumulate such loans and the scale to package the loans themselves.

In other words, I had been right that there were operational diseconomies for a national builder, but I had been wrong in not perceiving that the financial advantages from selling shares to the public would outweigh them. That change in the relative efficiency of the two types of companies was less important than the unprecedented way in which general economic and financial conditions since the late 1980s have favored all home builders. There has never before been such a long period of sustained effective demand to buy houses. Heretofore, the main differences in annual production of housing had been in rental units. But the steady increase in family formations, low mortgage rates, variable-rate loans, reduced down payments, liberalized mortgage qualifying standards, tax advantages, and unrestricted refinancing combined to create a self-fulfilling prophecy. Owning a home became desirable not just for having a place to live but also as an investment. For the first time, the single most important underpinning to consumer demand became money acquired by refinancing homes.

The result of all this has been an uninterrupted and accelerating increase in home prices. Most of this constitutes a rise in the value of land. Forty years ago when Kaufman and Broad went public, it emphasized its policy of treating land like other factors of production and inventorying very little of it. Pulte adopted a similar policy in the mid-1970s. In both cases, there had been recent periods in which too much housing was built. Reduced construction led to a recession, and builders with limited capital found themselves in deep trouble. But under the new circumstances cited above, home builders could not maintain such a policy. In fact, much of the very healthy profits that they have been making are caused by house prices rising during the time it takes to have a completed house for sale after they buy land. These increases in residual value more than made up for rising operating costs. The only offset to that difference is the cost of the money required to buy and hold the land. Since public companies have cheaper capital than their smaller, local competitors, they can either outbid them for raw land or make a larger gross profit on their houses, or both.

The only downside to this rosy scenario is the possibility that there is a bubble in housing prices. One cannot be certain about this, but it is clear that increases in housing prices over the last several years have outstripped rises in income or rents. In fact, in many instances rents have actually fallen. Furthermore, there is anecdotal evidence that many people are buying a house not to live in it but to rent it with the expectation that their capital gain will sufficiently exceed the inherent negative cash by enough to return a good profit. What is worse, some of them are borrowing on the equity in the house they occupy to raise the funds to do this. If there is a mild decline in house prices or even just a flattening, it could have two serious consequences. First, while public merchant builders will not experience a debt squeeze because they don't borrow much, their sales will slow and their margins will fall. The drop in sales will occur both for new homes and for resales. As a result, shareholders, their direct employees, suppliers and subcontractors, mortgage companies, and real estate brokers will all suffer. Second, refinancing will decline sharply. As has recently happened in Britain and Australia, even a flattening or only a slight fall in house prices may dramatically lower consumer spending, with all the negative consequences to the economy as a whole which that entails.

Such a scenario would benefit public companies in the long run since they are in a better financial position to weather these troubles than their smaller competitors. In fact, that trend may have been established when equivalent circumstances from 1973 to 1982 hurt all home builders but weeded out the weakest among them. Thirty years ago public companies accounted for only a tiny portion of all the houses built and sold in the United States. Today, the dozen or more that have survived have lifted that level to as much as 20 percent. Furthermore, as often occurs in bad times in any industry, there may be consolidation. However, that is unlikely seriously to reduce the cost of building houses or to improve them technologically. It will simply rationalize what has been a somewhat chaotic activity, a result that will not please those like myself who knew merchant building in its infancy. Back then, it was full of diverse and occasionally fascinating characters. Soon it may be run by colorless, but competent, managers.

Brands: Trump, Levitt, and Eichler

The names of each of these three men became a brand. For Bill Levitt and my father, it was attached to a particular kind of housing built from the late 1940s to the early 1960s. In one case, Levitt, the brand was creating entire communities in the Northeast that were occupied primarily by young, working- and lower-class, first-time buyers. In the other, Eichler, it was for building houses of contemporary design in medium-sized tracts in the San Francisco Bay Area. Trump had no such vision. The use of his buildings varied from hotels to casinos to offices to rental units to condominiums. For my father and Bill Levitt, fame flowed from their accomplishments. At least as early as 1974, when the then twenty-nine-year-old Donald Trump first called me, his overriding objective was to make himself a brand. Whatever he built or bought was to serve that purpose.

The personal failures of Bill Levitt and my father occurred for the same reasons. However much they enjoyed that fame, as well as the money that accompanied it, neither understood how to capitalize on it. As mentioned earlier, for Levitt it would have meant building more Levittowns of similar size and price range as those in New York, New Jersey, and Pennsylvania but targeted at a different customer, seniors, who in many cases could be the parents of his Northeast buyers. Ironically after much iteration in its ownership and name, the company he founded as Levitt and Sons is once again public, carries the original name, and caters to retirees, many of whom once lived in one of the three original Levittowns. In fact, they often say to the salesman, "I hope this is the same company that built Levittowns. I used to live in one."

For my father, the manner of capitalizing on the Eichler brand would, of course, have had to be different and less ambitious. It would have meant deviations from two design criteria he had embraced. One was setting the house close to the level of its site by using a concrete slab. The other was having the fixed glass areas sit directly on the slab. As a practical matter, these mandated a radiant heat system and made it almost impossible to air-condition the house. Furthermore, it made it very inflexible. For example, the ranges were all electric, and gas lines were only in the garage to provide fuel to heat the water in the two tanks that supplied it for general household use and radiant heat. When, as in my own case, people later decided they preferred to cook on a gas range top, it was difficult to make the change. After acting as CFO for the mortgage company I founded for ten years, my son, Steven, has decided to start his own business in Menlo Park, California, offering products and construction and design services for existing homes, many of which are of the same vintage and sell for about the same price as an Eichler home. Within a thirty-minute drive from his office, there are at least six thousand Eichlers, one of which he has been hired to remodel. As much as he likes the designs, he knows that there are far fewer alternatives for updating them than for conventional houses built on wood subfloors, which do not have large fixed glass areas running to the floor.

Concerned that these problems would arise someday and that they were already limiting our market, in 1961 I suggested to my father that we consider making two changes: switch to wood subfloors and construct a twelve-inch to eighteen-inch square box at the base of the outside walls on which fixed glass would sit and along some other interior walls. They would provide a channel for ducts for a combined heating and air-conditioning system or for pipes for water, baseboard heating, or both. The wood subfloor would provide additional space for pipes or ducts, as well as access to gas, plumbing, and electric lines. Another disadvantage of a radiant-heated slab is that it cannot be covered by a hardwood floor. Our architects at the time bragged about the flexibility of their designs. To the degree to which that applies to furniture placement, they may have been right, but I thought then and feel more strongly now that the aesthetic sacrifice, if there was one, was not worth the limitations.

Even without these changes in design, had my father not taken his company public or diversified, he could have continued building a few hundred Eichler homes in Marin, San Mateo, and Santa Clara Counties for some time and gradually turned the business over to me if he wanted it to survive him. Even if buyers would have had to pay some premium for the design, the power of the brand would probably have overcome the price difference, but it was not in his nature to do either. Ironically, in the end, his inability to take my feelings and ambitions into account was a boon for me. When I told Victor Palmieri that I wanted to be a home builder, I spoke the truth as I knew it, but I was wrong. I should have admired my father for his positive attributes—his sense of humor, his single-minded determination to build houses of superior design, and his belief in the role of government and the special responsibility of Jews—and accepted the faults that were inherent in these virtues. He was too involved in serving his own needs to consider what his son was really like. But then he never suggested that he could. After Eichler Homes went bankrupt, at the age of thirty-seven, I was forced to begin the long process of finding the answer to that question for myself.

When he contended that one man was far better than another at some activity, my father often said, "He can't hold a glove to..." That expresses my view of the character of Donald Trump as compared to that of Bill Levitt or my father. Whatever talent he has, he used entirely to make himself famous. He has no personal code. It is possible that as I conclude this book, a thorough analysis of his finances might show that the value of his debts exceed that of his assets. He has alienated his father and brothers, and I would be surprised if there is much, if anything, good to say about him as a father. One might forgive these failings if he had done anything of lasting value. I doubt that a few casinos, hotels, condos, and office buildings, whose only distinction is that they are pretentious, meet that test. He has not built a single building to match the distinctive character of the Seagrams or Chrysler buildings in New York, nor any complex as grand as Rockefeller Center. Every building he has built would never be noticed except for its carrying the name Trump, and a decade or two from now the value of it may have faded into oblivion. The last stages of the lives of my father and Bill Levitt deserve to be called tragic, whereas all of Donald Trump's adult life is closer to farce. Nevertheless I am grateful to him for two reasons. First, when times were unfavorable, he gave the Penn Central real estate disposition in New York a jump start. Second, had I not known him, I might not have thought of writing this book. How is that for fate?

11

Ned's Last Ventures: Mortgage Banking and Retirement

After leaving Levitt and New York in mid-1979, I returned to the Bay Area, taught for a semester at the Business School at UC–Berkeley, and wrote _The Merchant Builders_. Concurrently I began to consider how I might earn some money. Since I had received a substantial lump sum payment as my share of the VPCO incentive fee for the conclusion of the Levitt trusteeship, I was less concerned about the near term than about the future. I looked for a niche, one that would suit my unusual temperament and skills. An accident led me to one.

Early in 1981, I got a telephone call from Leo Dignan, the chief lending officer of St. Paul Federal Savings Bank of Illinois. He wanted my advice. He and his bank had been the sole lender for our home buyers in the Chicago area during my tenure at Levitt. St. Paul was a federally chartered, mutual thrift. Technically the depositors owned the company, but as a practical matter the board and the management were self-perpetuating. For example, the two top officers, the president and Dignan, had been with the company for twenty-five and thirty-five years, respectively, and had never held another job. Their business had been eminently simple. They garnered deposits upon which they paid interest, and they made home loans. Until Congress changed the rules in 1980, the interest rate they could pay depositors was set by the government, with the important exception of deposits over a certain size and beyond a certain time. As inflation began to increase in the late 1970s, so did interest rates. Simultaneously, thrifts and commercial banks had to compete with a new kind of institution, money market funds, whose deposit interest rates were not regulated. The dilemma for thrifts was twofold. First and foremost, they had large portfolios of single-family mortgages on which the interest rate was fixed at low interest rates. Second, every time they made a new loan, the rate would be at or even below their cost of funds. In

1980, this led Congress to lift the ceiling on deposit interest rates. In 1982, it removed the restrictions on what kind of investments they could make. In response, many of them made risky loans. With a few small exceptions, St. Paul had not done this. Its problem was that income on its existing portfolio was insufficient to cover its cost of funds. If it tried to set the rate on new loans high enough to offset this negative spread, it would be unable to find borrowers.

By 1981, many of the then 4,000 thrifts were in the same dilemma as St. Paul. Some decided to cease making long-term home loans and lend on high-yielding construction and development loans. I asked the owner and president of a Florida savings and loan, an ex–New Yorker, if he would let my company make apartment loans for him in California. He replied, "I will never make another loan. Under the new regs, I can sell Treasury bills [insured deposits] and invest in any deal I want. Hell, I could buy a deli on 6th Avenue in Manhattan." When I asked what kind of investments he intended to make, he said, "I am going to do joint ventures with developers." A great many thrifts took a similar route. The result was massive losses, much of them borne by the federal government.

Fortunately, St. Paul had not yet taken such risks, although Leo was considering them. I discouraged him and the president from doing that and spent about six months trying to devise a strategy by which they could find a profitable outlet for their money without taking inordinate risk. I explained that a few California thrifts had begun to market ARM loans to home buyers, but they correctly stated that Midwestern home owners would view such a product as too radical for them. Furthermore, they had concentrated on lending to customers of merchant builders, and demand for new housing in the Chicago area had almost collapsed. It was at this juncture that being an intellectual and an outsider served me well. After much thought and exploration, I concluded that there was a confluence of three circumstances peculiar to California, which together opened an opportunity for making reasonably safe ARM loans on existing apartment projects. First, after several years of apartment overbuilding in the state, especially in the Bay Area, the success of the environmental movement had greatly restricted new development approvals. By 1975, vacancies had disappeared and rents, which had been level or declining, began to rise. Second, under State Proposition 13, passed in 1978, property taxes could be raised only by a small fraction unless there was a sale. Thus, local government assessors could not capture a share of the increased values of rental properties unless they were sold. And third, the State Supreme Court ruled that the standard clauses in home or apartment loans that allowed the lender to call them if there is a sale or an additional encumbrance (a second mortgage) could be enforced in the event of a sale but not the addition of junior debt. There was an additional fact applicable throughout the United States, not just in California. Each year, owners of investment property can and do depreciate the physical improvements on an accelerated schedule for income tax purposes. However, when they sell the property, the IRS recaptures by using the depreciated basis as the cost of sales.

These four factors established an unusual and even counterintuitive lending opportunity. They allowed owners to "monetize" (acquire cash) some of their equity free of income taxes and without triggering an increase in property taxes by refinancing rather than selling. In addition, they could take advantage of the low interest rate on their old, first mortgage by leaving it in place and procuring a second mortgage. The conventional wisdom in lending was that seconds are riskier than firsts. However, I devised an underwriting method under which the reverse would be true. First, St. Paul could treat the two mortgages as a package and set a loan-to-value ratio of the total of both at a maximum of 75 percent. It could set the debt service cover in the same way. Since the firsts were old and had low interest rates, the percentage of the monthly payment allocated to principal was much higher than on a new loan. Thus, each month the total debt was being reduced faster than if all the debt were in a new first.

After I educated Dignan and his boss to these anomalies, they agreed to initiate a trial program. At the time, the interest on a twenty-five- or thirty-year fixed-rate loan was about 12 percent. I proposed the following terms for an ARM apartment second in California: term, ten years; frequency of rate change, six months; index, the six-month Treasury bill; initial rate, 2 percent under the fixed rate; interest rate cap for the term of the loan, 4 percent above the initial rate; interim interest rate cap, none; loan amounts, $500,000 to $5 million. I said that I would be in charge of getting the loans originated for a fee of 1 percent of the loan amount and would service the loans for a fee of one-eighth of 1 percent. Both of these fees were standard for the industry. I further suggested that St. Paul and I should conduct a trial with $20 million, which would mean ten to fifteen loans. If it succeeded, I proposed that they allocate at least $100 million per year thereafter. I knew that a major unanswered question was how prospective borrowers would respond to an ARM, even though I was convinced that this was a rare instance in which the terms benefited both the borrower and the lender.

Having never been in the lending business and having had few dealings with mortgage brokers, I assumed that they would be the channel for most of the loan originations. I was willing to let them have all or most of the origination fee. My main purpose was to capture the servicing fee. I knew that there were substantial economies of scale in loan servicing and wanted to establish for myself a dependable stream of future income. My assumptions about the usefulness of mortgage brokers turned out to be wholly inaccurate. I set up exclusive agencies in three sections of the Bay Area and set out to find candidates. There was no shortage of contenders, and all of them were thrilled to be able to offer a second mortgage at such favorable rates and terms. After three months, I had not received a single application. I then asked the broker who was handling Santa Clara County, which should have been the best market area, what was wrong. "What exactly do you say when you first talk to a prospect?" I asked.

"I present a 'menu' of all my loan programs," he replied. I then asked how they responded to ours, and he replied, "They love the idea of the second so they can keep their low interest rate from the first, and they like the rates, but they are afraid of the ARM provision." I asked if he explained that the rate could rise only by 2 percent above the current fixed rate, while there was no floor on how much it could go down. He said he did not, that he saw no point in trying to change a prospective borrower's mind. Somewhat surprised at this response, I asked him if he would consider an ARM loan if he were refinancing a rental project he owned. He said he would not.

The above experience suggested that I was in a situation similar to one my father and then I had sometimes faced thirty years earlier at Eichler Homes. I was trying to market an unconventional product through salespeople who themselves did not believe in its virtues. I now knew that I and/or my agent were going to have to meet with the prospect directly. I asked my brother-in-law, Art Thomas, who had sold computers and then houses, to join me as a partner. We soon discovered an obstacle that we had not considered. I knew how to find developers of houses and/or apartments, and I knew that most of them were quite well versed in financing. But as I established the parameters for our ideal borrower, I learned that few of them had ever been developers. They were owners who were highly skilled at acquiring and managing rental projects, but they were extremely difficult to locate and unsophisticated about financing.

I had constructed a simple scale from one to ten for rating the tenancy of apartments by income and social class. A rating of one was low and ten was high. I decided that we should target properties in the middle, from four to eight. The lower levels would present too many management problems for an owner because of transiency and collection difficulties, and the nines and tens were often the exclusive target of life insurance companies, who had a lower cost of funds than thrifts and who were adding to risk by outbidding each other in loan amounts. Often their chief lending officers and even some general officers took friends and wives out to show them "the beautiful project we had just financed." I set a rule for myself and St. Paul. We would not lend on any project in which I would want to live. A few years later, a former colleague at VPCO was consulting for a large insurance company, which was plagued with losses on apartment loans. He asked me to attend a meeting with them. I sat in a room with a dozen or so young men in their twenties and two senior loan officers and listened to them describe their plight. Finally I addressed one of the youngsters. "We lend on middle-income, boring properties in solid but not fancy locations and we have had no losses." I then asked him to give me the loan amount and the operating numbers on one of the properties they had taken over. I did a simple underwriting on it and said, "No wonder you have losses. Your loan is almost a million dollars higher than the amount we would use."

He replied, "Sure, you don't have to push the loan amount because you are not competing with other insurance companies for the business. You lend on lower-grade properties."

I then asked, "If we can do that, why can't you? You have a lower cost of funds than we do." There was no response.

As we investigated the issue, Art and I understood how difficult it was going to be to find our kind of owner. If we asked resident managers who they were, they would not tell us. We got records on microfiche cards, but most of the ownerships were partnerships in which the names of the partners were not shown. The partnership name would be something like "Page Mill Associates." I decided to approach the matter in two ways. One was to run small but striking ads in the local edition of the *Wall Street Journal.* I hired a cartoonist and described some comic scenes, each of which would emphasize ill treatment by a large lending institution. One showed a prospective borrower on his knees before a fat, ugly man sitting at a desk, smoking a big cigar and wearing a giant ring. The caption was, "You call that begging?" Another showed a supplicant sitting at a table across from a loan officer with forms piled almost to the ceiling. The caption was, "We just need you to fill out a few simple forms." Our other approach was to create a list and mail it first-class every month. I composed the letters in which I outlined our loan program, explained why an ARM was preferable to fixed-rate loan, and discussed the current economic and financial situation. Each time we made contact with a prospective buyer, even if it was clear that there was not a fit, we tried to get a referral from him. Knowing the power of the name Eichler, I used it for my company.

Our first loan came in part by another accident. In mid-afternoon on a Friday, the phone rang and I answered. A man said, "I saw your ad, but I want a fixed-rate loan." I decided to avoid the issue and asked him about the property. Obviously very proud of his accomplishments, he told me his story. He and his partner had been officers in Vietnam, lived in other parts of the country, liked the Bay Area when they came through it, settled here when they were discharged, bought a duplex and fixed it up for sale, expanded, and now owned six properties in San Francisco. Theirs were three-story buildings with commercial businesses on the first floor and apartments above in an excellent location. I then asked him what he was doing in the next hour or two and he said nothing.

Aware that he was very proud of what he and his partner had done, I said, "Suppose I come to your office and you show me all the properties." He agreed, told me his name was Bob Lytell, and gave me the tour. I learned that all the loans on these properties had been made by Golden West Savings. I knew not only its owners but also its chief lending officer, Ivan Chou.

When we got back to his office, I went to a big easel and asked Lytell to give me the income/expense numbers, the loan amounts, and the interest rates for each of the properties we had seen. When he did, I wrote them on the easel, estimated the loan amounts we could give him on each property, outlined our loan terms, and told him what his net proceeds would be from our refinancing. As he was pondering this information, Ivan Chou walked in. Lytell pointed to the easel and said, "That's the loans Ned can make us. What do you think of his deal?"

To his credit, Chou said, "It's a good deal, and I can't match it. If you want to have more money to buy other properties, you ought to do it." We did the package, a total of $6 million. Over the next three years we did another $25 million with the same borrowers. Against my advice, Lytell later bought larger, more diverse, and riskier properties, had losses, and went broke, but this did not affect the loans we had done for him.

As I got more into the business, I learned that our borrowers were very different from the developers I had known. I have already mentioned two of the ways. They were very private and ill-informed about financing and did not know how to think about it. Most of the initial contacts with them came by telephone calls from them to us in response to an ad, a mailing, or the suggestion of a friend. Usually the caller's first question was, "What's your program?" At first, I answered the question, but soon I realized that that was not the right tactic. I developed a list of five qualifying questions that I asked immediately: How many units is your property? Where is it? What is the amount of the existing loan? What is your net income? What size loan are you seeking? The answer to any of these questions would indicate whether we could even consider the loan. If that was the case, it was better for both of us to know it right away. I adopted this method not just to save my time or Art's but also to convey a message to the borrower that we did not want to waste his time. If the property seemed to qualify, I would outline our loan terms. More often than not, prospects would initially be wary of an ARM, but I found that over time, sometimes only after ten or even twenty telephone conversations in which the same ground was covered, many of them could be converted to a product I believed was better for them than a fixed-rate loan.

As I had anticipated, interest rates fell. Concurrently, the principal balances of old firsts were becoming too low to mean much. Therefore, seconds became less desirable for borrowers, and we shifted our emphasis to firsts. In the five years from mid-1982 to mid-1987, we originated over $750 million in loans for St. Paul, which constituted at least 50 percent of its total lending. Then its board decided to follow a general trend and abandon its status as a mutual company and issue publicly traded stock. The success of our efforts had made this possible, but being so dependent on the services of an outside firm would not be acceptable to security underwriters. I had gone a long way toward accomplishing my goal of building a substantial servicing income, but I knew that loan amortization and early payoffs, as well, of course, as the ten-year term, would result in a decrease and ultimate end to it. I tried to find another funding source, but the best I could do was a smaller Chicago thrift, Cragin Federal, which was willing to allocate only $60 million a year. I decided to turn the day-to-day management over to Art so that I could spend more time on completing the Ph.D. courses and writing *The Thrift Debacle*.

I encountered several interesting borrowers in those five years, but two stand out to me today. All lenders, including St. Paul, had what I thought was a silly requirement for a borrower who was refinancing to monetize his equity. They wanted him to declare what he was going to do with the proceeds. Of course, if one wanted to use the money to buy another property, we were more than willing to try to make a loan for that too. But it had nothing to do with the safety of the loan being considered. Still, we had to comply. One day Art rushed into my office and said, "I just heard a great answer to that question about the use of proceeds."

"What was it?" I asked.

Arthur replied, "This guy is in his late sixties and owns three other properties that are performing very well. When I asked what he was going to do with the proceeds, he said he was going to take the money he gets from this loan, go to Las Vegas, and 'piss it away.'"

When I stopped laughing, I said to Arthur, "What a great answer. We ought to give the guy a break on the fee." Needless to say we told him we would need a more benign reason for the lender.

The other was a Korean named Sing Hahn, who preferred to be called Sam and whom I got to know quite well. He had come to the United States thirty years earlier with his wife to attend the University of Texas. When he graduated with an accounting degree, he was offered a job with JC Penney at $25,000 per year, but he told his wife that this was not what he really wanted to do. She asked what that was and he said, "I want to own and manage apartment projects." He went on to tell her that he could borrow some money from his parents in Korea to get started and knew it was a risk, and he asked how she felt about the idea. She said he should follow his dream. He studied the whole country and settled on Santa Clara County. When I met him, he owned well over a thousand units in five projects, had no debt other than mortgages on these properties, had $2.5 million in a savings account at Bank of America, lived in a very nice house, drove a Mercedes, and had five children, all of whom were at or had graduated from MIT. Three of the children were accomplished musicians. Over the following year, we made five loans to him at a total of about $30 million.

Sam was the best apartment operator I ever met. Because the annual turnover in mid-priced, suburban, garden apartments ranges from 50 to 100 percent, it is impossible for an owner to have total economic occupancy. Each time a tenant moves, the unit has to be repainted and refurbished. The most efficient owners I knew in a strong rental market could achieve only an effective 97 percent occupancy. By running his own painting and cleaning crews and possessing a maniacal attention to detail, he got his projects up to 98.5 percent. Sam had a unique complaint about his wife, whom I had met and found very attractive. He could not get her to spend enough money on clothes or other items for herself. "I keep telling her to go to nice stores, but she won't do it. She shops at JC Penney."

Two years after we made the loans to Sam, he called me to ask my opinion on an offer he had from a life insurance company to replace the ARMs with loans fixed at an 11 percent interest rate for seven years. At the time, his rate on our loans was 9 percent, the cap was 13 percent, and the remaining term was eight years. Clearly, I had a vested interest in retaining the servicing of Sam's loans and told him so. But I also believed and said that he would make a mistake by accepting the new offer. I reminded him that he could repay our loan at any time without penalty, whereas the insurance company's fixed-rate loans had a lock-in provision that precluded prepayment until the last year of the term. I went on to give my opinion that interest rates would continue to fall and to remind him that the rate on our loan could not exceed 13 percent, only 2 percent higher than the new rate he would be getting. Two weeks later he called to tell me had decided to go ahead with the insurance company refinance. After another two years passed, interest rates had in fact gone down, and in great dismay Sam called me again. He said, "You were right. I should not have taken the insurance company loans. How can I pay them off?" I told him he could not. I saw and/or talked with him several times in the subsequent years and made several more loans to him. After telling me the latest positive news about his children and complaining about his wife's thriftiness, he always concluded by saying, "You were right, Ned."

In 1987, a borrower asked if we would process a loan for him with Fannie Mae. I had experimented with submitting loans to the other agency, Freddie Mac, and found the system too difficult for my purposes. With St. Paul, we could fix the loan rate at application, make ARM loans, and, if required, close in two or three weeks from the date of application. With Freddie Mac and later Fannie Mae, the rate was fixed only at closing, which could take as long as four months. However, because Cragin had limited the number of loans we could make, our processors had extra time, and I decided to see if things would be any better at Fannie Mae. They were not. Fannie Mae operated through five regional offices. The one for the West was in Pasadena. It had adopted standards much like those of life insurance companies. It would not approve a loan for a property that had any asbestos, a fact of which I was unaware until the loan had been processed by them for two months. I too would require the removal of pipe or duct wrapping containing asbestos. But from the 1950s until well into the 1970s, the ceiling in most houses and apartment complexes built in California had been "shot" (covered) with material that looked like plaster and contained small amounts of asbestos. On the other hand, in contrast to residential construction in the Midwest and the East, the water pipes, boilers, furnaces, and ducts were not wrapped at all. Independent environmental consultants issued reports in which they noted the asbestos in ceilings but did not require or even recommend removal. Instead, they prescribed a simple maintenance program, which all professional apartment owners and managers followed anyway and which the thrifts and commercial banks accepted.

In late 1988, Hal Potter, the loan officer at Fannie Mae in Pasadena, called me to ask if I would consider joining a small group of mortgage bankers who were participating in a new Fannie Mae apartment lending program. It was called DUS, which stood for "Delegated Underwriting and Servicing." Under it, if the lender (us) agrees to follow specific underwriting guidelines *and* share in the credit risk, he can process and close the loan without prior approval and get a higher servicing fee. In effect, the mortgage banker is selling risk insurance. For the benefit of greater control over the process, especially speed, and a higher servicing fee, the lender insures Fannie Mae against loss. HUD had had significant losses in an earlier program. Fannie Mae had tried to learn from this experience and adopt more restrictive rules in four important ways. First, it was selective about who could join the program. Second, it required the mortgage banker to have considerable capital and to deposit one-half of 1 percent of each loan amount in a special account. Third, it adopted very detailed and more restrictive underwriting rules. And fourth, it inspected every property and underwriting package shortly after closing. If it found violations, it could increase the lender's share of the risk and/or remove him from the program.

I asked Potter why he was inviting me to participate. He said that Fannie Mae had bought some of the loans I had originated for St. Paul and liked their quality. Also, even though a DUS member could lend anywhere in the country, Fannie Mae was trying to have representation in major markets. It had it in southern California but not in the Bay Area. He told me the capital requirement was $2.5 million and that I could not count the value of our servicing toward it. Bankers Mutual, with whom we had competed for some loans, was the southern California member. I asked him for a list of the others with contact names and telephone numbers. I then reminded him of the problem we had had with the one loan we had submitted to Fannie Mae's prior approval program, and I asked if the property standards, including the restriction against shot ceilings, obtained. He said the standards were lower for DUS because the lenders were at risk. I asked him to come to the Bay Area to see a specific property so I could find out more precisely what the standard would be. When he came, I showed him a thirty-year-old apartment project in a solid location with lower-middle- and working-class tenants. In my scale, it was a 5 or a 6 and had shot ceilings. He said that it fit the DUS program but that he would reject it for prior approval.

Not having the required capita or any idea of how to raise it, I contacted the owner of Bankers Mutual to see if he was interested in a partnership in which we would make loans only in the Bay Area. He said he was, and we met at his office. As he described his method of operation, I became troubled. He presented his company to prospective borrowers as a private bank and did not tell them that the funds came from Fannie Mae. His main reason for doing this was to get higher fees and explained how he did that. Fannie Mae set its closing interest rate to two decimal points. For example, its rate on a given day might be 9.51 percent. A DUS lender could pass that rate on to the borrower or, if he choose, round the rate up to the next quarter, in this example to 9.75 percent, and add the difference of 0.24 percent to the allowed 0.25 percent servicing fee. As I indicated above, I got a lot of repeat and referred business by giving good service and telling borrowers all the relevant facts about our loan program. I had no intention of abandoning that practice and by omission deceiving a borrower. In fact, I saw that I could gain a competitive edge with Bankers Mutual in the program. Later Fannie Mae raised its initial capital requirement to $7.5 million and its standard servicing fee to 0.5 percent and banned lenders from rounding up the daily rate.

When I received the list of other DUS lenders, I was about to leave for New York to give a lecture and noticed that one of the members was located there. Its name was PW Funding. I knew that in contrast to most of the rest of the country, New York mortgage bankers were often Jewish. I assumed that the initials were the first letters of the last names of two partners, who, like Marty Gleich and Harvey Furgatch (see Chapter VIII), used a more neutral name. I could not have been more wrong. When I called and asked to speak to a partner, I was directed to John Marr. I soon learned that the company had been a subsidiary of Paine Webber, had specialized in FHA-insured hospital loans, and had been bought by the two men who ran it: Marr, the vice president, and Ray Reisert, the president, who had formerly been a hospital administrator. Paine Webber had become concerned about the potential for losses from the hospital loans, had left $4 million in the company in nonvoting, preferred stock, and had sold the common stock to Marr and Reisert for a modest sum. The capital base met the DUS requirement, and a year earlier they had become a member largely because recent restrictions in FHA underwriting standards had limited their ability to make hospital loans. Marr knew something about commercial real estate from his days as a construction lender for City Corp. Reisert had no experience with it. In the year after they joined the DUS program, they had made one $15 million loan on property in Chicago, which was not performing well.

When I went to their office on 7th Avenue, I was immediately struck by how spacious and sumptuous it was. If, as I believed, the DUS program most suited modest-sized, suburban apartment projects, if the borrowers rarely lived in a central city, and if most of the face-to-face contact with them was at their offices, there was no reason to put on a big show at great expense for them. Our office rent was less than 20 percent of theirs and we did far more business. Reisert was out of town and Marr was and is a very congenial man. As we talked, I had an idea. I asked him if we might structure a joint venture under which we would originate and service DUS loans in California and, in effect, rent PW's DUS license. He expressed interest and asked how that might work. I suggested a two-year agreement under which we would split 50/50 the origination and servicing fees and share the risk. I would bear all out-of-pocket costs of both functions from my share. He asked me what I thought the average loan size would be and how much volume we might. I estimated the loan size at $3 to $4 million and annual volume at $200 million. A few weeks later, Reisert came to review our operation and inspect properties, liked what he saw, and agreed to my proposal. We sought and gained Fannie Mae approval of the only arrangement of its kind in the DUS system.

Art had left my company but at my request came back to work solely on originations. We were a good team. Borrowers liked and trusted him as a person. When he had a reluctant prospect, I went with him to add weight. As it happened, this circumstance arose as soon as we started marketing the DUS program. Art had a prospect who was not quite typical of our borrowers in that he was both a developer and an owner. He had recently finished the rent-up of three newly built projects, which on my scale were 8s, and wanted to put permanent, fixed-rate loans on them. He had two concerns. First, he equated Fannie Mae with HUD, with whom he had had a bad experience. Second, we had closed a lot of loans but none with Fannie Mae. As we drove to his office in San Jose to meet him, Art told me that the man was about to go into the hospital for an operation, which was not life-threatening but from which it would take him several weeks to recuperate. When we met, he repeated what I already knew and said, "I don't want to give you $30,000 for the cost of appraisal, engineering, and environmental reports and find out I had wasted my money and time, especially for a loan program that is brand-new to you." The Fannie Mae interest rate was not set until approval, which would take thirty to forty-five days. I asked him what rate would be acceptable to him. He said 9.5 percent, although clearly he would have liked it to be lower.

I then made the following proposal to him. "You get your operation. Before you go in the hospital, tell your son, whom I just met, to provide us with all the information we need to process the three loans. Art has already given you a list of what we need. I will advance the $30,000 for the three reports. In no more than forty-five days, which will about coincide with your expected time for recuperation, if we have approval for the loan amounts you set, and the interest rate is at or below 9.5 percent, you will close and reimburse us for the cost of the reports. If not, it will be my loss." He agreed and we left.

As I was making this proposal, I saw Art turn white. When we were alone in the car, he erupted. "How could you be so foolish?" he asked.

I said, "Look at this from his point of view. We haven't done a DUS loan. Why should he trust us? The more I tell him how sure I am that he will get the loan amount and the interest rate he wants, the more he is going to say it is just a sales pitch. He has heard that crap from a zillion mortgage brokers and, understandably, he puts us in the same category."

Needless to say, we met the terms of our agreement, and he closed at 9 percent. Not only had I gotten the new program off to a good start, but I had added a great prospect who would give us more business and referrals. That was the first step of a very successful year. We closed over $400 million, 25 percent of which came from three borrowers. One of them was a former classical musician, who had accumulated apartments in southern California and then sold them. He used the proceeds to buy nine complexes in Sacramento. He had called three years earlier to ask if I would make a $2.5 million loan on one of his properties there. I got the numbers, looked at it the next day, and called him back to say that I could not go higher than $2 million. He thanked me for the prompt reply but said that was not enough money. I had forgotten about the incident, but in 1989 he called again and said, "I never forgot how well you treated me. Most mortgage brokers or lenders 'sandbag' you. They tell you they can get a certain amount. You pay for reports and sixty days later they say, 'Gee, I couldn't quite get what you want, but it is still a good deal.' I hate that and so do most other owners. So now I want to refinance all nine of my properties in Sacramento with new firsts to lock up current rates. The loans will total about $40 million."

In several respects, I applied my experience at merchant building to my mortgage business. I examined every step in processing a loan in order to accomplish three purposes. The first was to have both high quality and fast processing. The second was to keep the costs to me and to the borrower to a minimum. The third was regularly to inform the prospective borrower of the status of his loan. I shall give some examples of specific ways in which I met these goals. I knew that even though borrowers would often say they were in a hurry to close, they hated filling out forms and often had sloppy records. I treated the steps in processing a loan as two parallel assembly lines. One was to gather the required information from the borrower. The other was to move forward four outside services, the three reports cited above and a legal opinion. For the former, I sought processors who were willing and able to act as sheep herders or, as I often put it, "pests." To accomplish this, I paid about 30 percent more than the going rate for the work. I often said to a new employee, usually a woman, "I'll tell you what will constitute success in this job. It's when we have funded a loan and the borrower says to me, 'That Goddamn woman was a terrible pest. She was on my ass every day for those Goddamn papers. Now, I want to know if you'll do another loan for me, and I'd like her to handle the processing.' I learned that it is almost impossible to insult our kind of borrower." When borrowers would not comply, I told the processor to say, "Okay, I am going to put your file at the end of the line." Fannie Mae required an elaborate narrative underwriting for each loan, much of which served no useful purpose. Much as I disapproved of this, I hired underwriters and instructed them to follow those requirements to the letter. When borrowers or underwriters asked me why there were so many silly rules, I said, "Why is for the minister or the rabbi. My job is to tell you 'what,' what you have to do to get the loan approved. Whether I think many of the requirements are irrational is imma- terial."

For the three reports, I sought modest-size companies so that I would be their biggest, but not their only, customer. I wanted the steady volume I could give them to result in low fees and good service. I said that as a standard practice I wanted the report within two weeks, but in a special case, where the borrower has a legitimate need for speed, I want it in a week at most. I had a further demand of appraisers. When an owner applied or even showed serious interest, if I was uncertain about what the appraised value might be, I wanted to be able to call the appraiser and ask him to inspect the property and give me his opinion. I said that I would not abuse this privilege, and I did not. I knew that the actual work for the reports took no more than two or three days. The issue was where our loans were put in their line. The legal opinion was similar in some respects but not in others. I did not want to of money for a skill that lawyers rarely possess: adminis- tration. I picked a pay a lot man whom I knew. He had recently left a big firm to start his own practice. I told him that in 19 out of 20 cases there would be no legal issue at all, but the opinion was a requirement. I said, "Our closing officer will collect all the information you need to issue an opinion, which usually means partnership documents and preliminary title reports, review them first for any obvious problems, and then send them to you. If you need more information, tell her, not the borrower or his lawyer. If you spot a serious problem, tell me. Since Fannie Mae notes and mortgages cannot be changed, we will instruct borrowers to tell that to their lawyer. If a borrower's lawyer calls you, refuse to talk to him. Many lenders permit their lawyers to make some changes. Fannie Mae does not. The borrower's lawyer also has to provide an opinion, which is redundant, but I don't want any unnecessary money spent by the borrower on legal fees." The standard fee for a lender's legal opinion was $5,000 to $10,000. I assured our lawyer that he would make good money at $1,500 per loan, as long as he fol- lowed my rules and charged more only in the rare case where there was a real issue. He agreed grudgingly but soon admitted that I was right.

Reisert and Marr, as well as most DUS lenders and other mortgage bankers, were amazed and even shocked at these methods, especially on the legal fees. When they asked me why I went to so much trouble to limit the borrower's costs, it demonstrated their irresponsibility both to the borrower and to themselves. He was our customer. Keeping his cost for third-party services down was both good for business and the responsible thing to do. I once got a phone call from a borrower's lawyer, who insisted that he be able to talk to our counsel. I asked why he wanted to do that. He said, "So that I can assure my client that the loan documents are okay."

I said, "If you have read the documents and it is your opinion that he should not sign them, you should tell him that and give him your reasons. The documents cannot be altered and I don't want your client to pay additional legal fees to you and our counsel to humor you. And if you call me or our counsel once more, I will cancel the loan."

Less than fifteen minutes later, the borrower called me and asked what I had said to get his lawyer so upset. I told him what had transpired. After a brief pause, he said, "You certainly are not a typical mortgage banker. I've done a lot of loans, and I never met someone in your business who was interested in saving my money. I hope I can do more loans with you and will pass this along to my friends."

To me, many of Fannie Mae's underwriting standards made no sense. One example was the headquarters overriding a provision of the Western regional office that a lender could waive the requirement that the borrower deposit large sums of money for reserves if past performance warranted doing so. The borrowers who were very attentive to making repairs and replacements resented the necessity of tying up large sums of money years before they would be needed for the project. On one occasion I met with Fannie Mae's headquarters staff to complain of this and about a dozen other unnecessary requirements. I got nowhere and made enemies. After the meeting, I was scheduled to have lunch with Tom White, then the head of the DUS program. I repeated my complaints to Tom, who was a former state legislator from Michigan and quite intelligent. On the reserve issue, Tom asked me what I would do if a prospective borrower had not kept up his property. I said I would not make the loan at all. "A reserve would not be enough to cure that kind of behavior," I said.

Tom replied, "I know that. You're the only DUS lender who knows how to say no, but I can't make the rules to fit you."

The door to his office was open and I looked out at the dozen or so staff members, pointed to them, and said, "So all those people are here to dream up rules to corral your most incompetent lenders, and I have to suffer the consequence."

Tom paused for a moment and then said, "That's right. You'll just have to live with it. Now, let's go get some lunch."

When the agreement with PW Funding ended after two years, Fannie Mae told us they did not want it to continue. They said we should merge or I should get my own license. Reisert and I explored the possibility of merging, but two factors prevented it. I was concerned about the potential for losses from his hospital loans, and he wanted control. However, after pursuing John Marr for four more years, I convinced him to join my company. He is still there. In Chapter IX, I told the story of how I found Harold Blumenstein and how he became an active financial partner in the second stage of my relationship with Fannie Mae. In the offering circular that he obtained, I projected annual origination volume at $200 million per year. Over the next four years, our volume at $1.4 billion was almost double that. I had stopped making loans in California and concentrated on the Southwest and other markets where rents and values had actually declined or at least had risen far less than in California. The competition was also less intense in these markets.

As stated earlier, I retired in 1996 and sold my share of the company's stock to Harold and his partner. The company has retained most of the managers and salespeople who were there then and, unlike other mortgage bankers, has continued to have only one source of funding, Fannie Mae. I knew that the stock was worth much more than the sale price, but I also knew that there was a risk, however small, to the portfolio. Harold tried to dissuade me from selling, but I had accomplished what I intended. I had created a successful company through unorthodox means that reflected my iconoclastic nature, but I had outlived my usefulness. As was inevitable, I had alienated several members of Fannie Mae's mid-level bureaucracy with whom we had to deal. We made Byron Steenerson president. He had been at best marginally successful at selling, but he was a competent manager and well liked at Fannie Mae. Since I left, annual origination volume has continued at about $400 million per year. Despite the offset of loan amortization and payoffs, the portfolio has more than doubled to over $3 billion. There were no defaults, late payments, or losses on the roughly $2 billion in loans that had been done with Fannie Mae during my tenure. Even later, there was only a handful. Clearly, I would have been much richer had I kept my stock, but I have no regret about that. By taking the payment over twenty years, I would have more than enough money for whatever I wanted for the rest of my life. I had seen the emotional difficulty of founders letting go. I did not want to repeat that pattern. I often told people who worked with and for me, "You have to be able to put your head on the pillow at night and say to yourself, 'I left some money on the table today, but I don't care. I did the best I could and succeeded well enough.'"

At the age of sixty-six, it was time for me to take my own advice. I wanted to have time to do more writing, perhaps of a different kind than I had done before. Of even more importance, there were activities in which I wanted to engage and explorations of my personal life which I wanted and needed to make. My parents and all the family members of their generation were dead. My brother, with whom I was estranged for most of our adult lives, would soon die broke. One of his three daughters had committed suicide, and the other two were leading marginal lives. Fortunately I have been able to help one of them realize at the age of forty-four a long-held desire to attend college and get a degree in teaching. I was on good terms with my two sons from the first marriage, but my daughter from the third marriage was finally trying to recover from a long bout of depression. After failing at marriage three times, I feared that I was unsuited for a deep and lasting relationship with a woman. Still, that was something I very much wanted. My wives had not had a profession nor were they highly educated. I decided that that was the problem and had successive affairs with the chair of a university art department, a nationally respected sociologist, and an acclaimed documentary filmmaker. None of them worked. However, with aid of a wonderful therapist, I came to understand what was really wrong with the women I had chosen.

For me, she had to have a large, generous heart and not be suspicious of and resentful toward men. When I was introduced to such a woman, Ava, by a friend, her presence did not immediately produce a spark. As I later told her, "I thought you were too conventional." But, fortunately for me, she understood why she and I might be right for each other. She was not looking to be saved or fixed. Rather, she wanted loyalty, warmth, sensuality, and companionship and sensed that that was what I wanted too. She was right. We were married almost four years ago, and for the first time (she had been married twice) each of us found communion in marriage. As a bonus, I became very close to her only daughter and granddaughter.

Periodically, Ava says to me, "We are so happy together. I wish we had met and married long ago so we could have had children of our own."

I always give the same reply: "I am not certain about you, but had I met you much earlier, I would not have had the sense to embrace the qualities which have endeared you to me. Only recently, and only after having all those failures and enduring considerable pain, did I realize what kind of woman was right for me."

Unlike Donald Trump, I had not sought fame, and unlike my father and Bill Levitt, I had not gained it, but, as I have used the word in this book, I have found fortune.

978-0-595-36734-4
0-595-36734-8

Printed in the United States
49180LVS00002BA/319-549

9 780595 367344